Communication of Migration in Media and Arts

Communication of Migration in Media and Arts

Edited by

Vildan Mahmutoğlu and John Morán González

TRANSNATIONAL PRESS LONDON
2020

Migration Series: 26

Communication of Migration in Media and Arts

Edited by Vildan Mahmutoğlu and John Morán González

Copyright © 2020 Transnational Press London

First Published in 2020 by TRANSNATIONAL PRESS LONDON in the United Kingdom, 12 Ridgeway Gardens, London, N6 5XR, UK.
www.tplondon.com

Requests for permission to reproduce material from this work should be sent to: sales@tplondon.com

Paperback
ISBN: 978-1-912997-65-7

Cover Design: Nihal Yazgan

www.tplondon.com

CONTENT

ABOUT AUTHORS

Vildan MAHMUTOĞLU is Associate Professor at Galatasaray University, Istanbul. Her research interests include migration, local cultures, gender and minorities. Her current research is about gender in diaspora. She has been an editor of Galatasaray University Communication faculty journal *İleti-ş-im* since January 2020.

John Morán GONZÁLEZ is the J. Frank Dobie Regents Professor of American and English Literature and Director of the Center for Mexican American Studies at the University of Texas at Austin. He has authored two monographs: *Border Renaissance: The Texas Centennial and the Emergence of Mexican American Literature* and *The Troubled Union: Expansionist Imperatives in Post-Reconstruction American Novels*. He is editor of *The Cambridge Companion to Latina/o American Literature* and co-editor (with Laura Lomas) of *The Cambridge History of Latina/o American Literature*. He is co-editor (with Sonia Hernández) of *Reverberations of Racial Violence: Critical Reflections on Borderlands History* (forthcoming 2021).

BALCA Arda is Department Chair and Assistant Professor of Visual Communication Design at Kadir Has University, Istanbul. Her dissertation "The Sublime in Contemporary Art and Politics: The post-9/11 Art of the Middle Eastern Diaspora in North America" (York University, Toronto - 2016), builds on aesthetic and communication theory together with ethnographic study in diasporic and postcolonial literatures. Her latest publications are "Contemporary Art on the Current Refugee Crisis: The Problematic of Aesthetics versus Ethics" (2019) in the *British Journal of Middle Eastern Studies* and "Cinematic Visual Representation of Refugee Journeys in Turkey in the Context of Precarious Class Dynamics" (2020) in *Migration Letters*. Balca worked as the illustrator for Davetsiz Misafir [The Uninvited Guest], an intellectual magazine of comics, science-fiction, cinema, and critique in Turkey. Her recent art exhibitions were in Cedar Ridge Gallery in Toronto and Gallery MCRD in Istanbul. She was awarded with Dwight Conquergood Award in 2019 by the Performance Studies International for her research with disenfranchised communities.

Gabriela ABRASOWICZ holds a Ph.D. in in Slavic Philology from Wrocław University. Her dissertation about contemporary women-dramatists in Serbia and Croatia was prepared under the supervision of Prof. Magdalena Koch. She is the author of *Body Drama, The Body in The Drama. The Work of Serbian and Croatian Women Playwrights in The Years 1990-2010* as well as a series of ariticles dealing with the question of analysis of post-Yugoslav drama writing and theatre from the perspective of anthropology of the body, gender studies, and transcultural studies. Presently, she is carrying out a research project titled, "(Trans)positions of Ideas in Croatian and Serbian Playwriting and Theatre (1990-2020): A Transcultural Perspective" under the auspices of the National Science Center, Poland.

Eric TRINKA (Ph.D., The Catholic University of America) is an award-winning biblical scholar who works at the intersections of the topics of religion and migration in both the ancient and modern worlds. He writes on the history of biblical composition, ancient Near Eastern history and religion, the use of the Bible in the modern world, and on a wide range of issues concerning the place of religion in the migration experience.

Bianca-Florentina CHEREGI is an Assistant Lecturer at the College of Communication and Public Relations at the National University of Political Studies and Public Administration in Bucharest, Romania. She is also a postdoctoral researcher on "Labour Market in the Fields of Intelligent Specialization," sponsored by the National University of Political Studies and Public Administration (CERT-ANTREP). She is also a program coordinator in Brand Management and Corporate Communication, and was a "Spiru Haret" fellow during academic year 2017-2018. Her latest publications include a monograph titled *Nation Branding in Post-Communist Romania. A semiotic approach* (comunicare.ro, 2018). Her published book chapters include "The Media Framing of Migration in Sending and Receiving Countries: The Case of Romanians Migrating to the UK" (London, Palgrave MacMillan, 2018), "Let's Change the Story!" - Nation Branding and Interactive Media Campaigns on Romanian Migration" (UK, Cambridge Scholars Publishing, 2017). Her academic interests include migration, media framing, nation branding, public diplomacy, digital ecosystem, country image, and visual semiotics.

Bilgen TÜRKAY is a first-year Ph.D. student at University of Cincinnati in the Political Science Department. She previously completed an M.A. in Journalism at Ankara University; her thesis topic was: "Syrian Refugees, Social Media and Civil Society: Integration Process and Seeking for Solutions." She has two undergraduate degrees in International Relations, and Public Relations and Advertisement, respectively. Her research interests are immigration, social media & technology, human rights, and national security.

Barış ÖKTEM is currently a Ph.D. candidate in Middle East Politics at the University of Exeter. Barış is completing a dissertation titled "Reformulation of Colonialism and Its Effects on Refugees: The Comparative Case of Syrian Refugees in Turkey, Greece and Germany." He obtained his bachelor's degree at Anadolu University in Turkey in 2012, and afterwards he was rewarded a full-time scholarship for graduate study abroad by the Turkish Ministry of Education. He earned a master's degree after studying Sociology at the University of Essex in 2016. His research was focused on the "Radical Democracy and Democratic Nation" concepts of a political representation, with a specific interest in political parties in Turkey. Barış has academic interests in colonialism, migration, Syrian refugees, social media studies, and Kurdish politics. He is a freelance journalist working for British Broadcasting Company (BBC), an amateur musician with interest in percussion instruments, and an active sportsman.

INTRODUCTION

Vildan Mahmutoğlu and John Moran Gonzalez

THE MAN: In the kitchen of the Thai/Chinese/Vietnamese restaurant
THE GOLDEN DRAGON: it's cramped, there's no room, but there are still five Asian cooks working here. One of them's got toothache: the boy, the one who's looking at his sister. The new one.
THE YOUNG WOMAN screams in pain.
THE MAN OVER SIXTY: We call him the boy.
THE YOUNG WOMAN: It hurts-
THE WOMAN OVER SIXTY: Toothache.
THE YOUNG WOMAN: Oh that hurts, it really hurts.
THE MAN OVER SIXTY: Don't scream, don't scream-
THE MAN: Screaming will use up your energy.
THE YOUNG MAN: We call him boy because he's new.
THE WOMAN OVER SIXTY: Because he's not been here so long. He's still new. And he's got no Money. And he's got no papers.
So a dentist is out of the question.
(Roland Schimmelpfennig, *The Golden Dragon*, 2009)

While the phenomenon of migration is as old as humanity itself, the contemporary world is defined by constant displacement and movement of people, whether caused by the economics of poverty or the politics of violence. Even in the case of migration for a better education and or working conditions, migrants often have difficulties when they arrive new "homeland". But if they leave as refugees and asylum-seekers, reception conditions are usually even worse due to the uncertainties of being recognized as such by receiving states. Taking a close look at the stories of migrants, with the help of case studies, shows that their experiences are no longer just the statistics of displacement, but rather make us to think of the human experience that migration is.

Most often, media shapes public opinion of migrants. On one hand, the media is heavily criticized because they provide only partial portraits. As such, it cannot create a public space for a deliberative democracy. Indeed, the main function of the traditional media is to provide information to the public, but today, traditional media cannot fulfill these expectations. The media gives information prejudicedly, shaping public opinion according to governmental dictates or in the interests of corporate elites. On the other hand, the formation of new media technologies, particularly those based upon data-enabled Internet mobile phones, at times sidesteps the problems of traditional media when used correctly. New social media, due to its interactive structure, intervenes in the public sphere in ways that traditional media may fail to do, focused as traditional media coverage of migration is on migrant criminality and abjection. In contrast, the daily lives of immigrants can be the subject of new media platforms. Social media, which is one of the important elements of new media, becomes a venue that migrants themselves use. The fact that the new media is fast, communicating events immediately, presenting them to the world beyond, even unto the groves of academia.

Like migration, art is as old as the history of civilization. It expresses the thoughts and emotions of the artist and also the great issues of the time, leaving traces in its content. The works created by artists with certain aesthetic concerns can tell the troubles and social events of the period. When it comes to the present day, it is impossible for the traces of migration not to pass into works of art such as *The Golden Dragon*. In this play, the German writer Roland Schimmelpfenning tells the story of immigration policies and human trafficking through a Thai-Chinese-Vietnamese fast food restaurant. This play, about a deceased migrant, depicts the consequences of human trafficking at the personal level. The immigrant boy has a terrible toothache but he cannot go to any doctor because of his undocumented status. The play takes place in an unnamed European city, and the immigrant boy's short life story can be seen in anywhere where there are asylum seekers.

In the symposium held at the British Museum in London on July 7, 2019, six Yemeni and four Syrian artists discussed what art is in the wrecked countries. One of them, Murad Subay, a Yemeni street artist, said he painted a mural about the arms industry because he focuses upon the destructiveness of guns. Another Yemeni, filmmaker Ibi Ibrahim, said that what he does is a basic need of society, creating art as a mirror to society at such times. Because art is not only a creation made with artistic concerns, but also because artists have to represent the troubles of society. Abraham added in his speech that democracy will also disappear where culture is destroyed. War destroys works of art and art institutions so it is evident that many foundations and museums endeavour to include the artists and works of the countries that are at war. In war-torn countries, institutions of art are inaccessible, if not destroyed. The use of the Internet at this stage can support the dissemination of art, overcoming spatial problems and constraints.

In this critical anthology, contributors examine migration, art, and the media in the contemporary migration studies to critically analyse their interactions and intersections. The chapters are grouped under two main headings: "Migration in Art" and "Migration and Media".

In Chapter One, "Representation of Asylum seekers in Science Fiction films: Prawns in District 9," Vildan Mahmutoglu lays out a brief history of the representation of asylum seekers in science fiction film, and then examines a contemporary instance through the South African science fiction film *District 9* (2009).

Chapter Two is Balca Arda's "Border Imagery and Refugee Abjection in Contemporary Visual Art". Arda's chapter explores contemporary visual art that aims to remedy the abjection of the migrant in nativist nationalist discourse by imagining citizens as refugees and refugees as citizens. Such an artistic reversal potentially imagines the interior frontier between "migrants" and "natives", yet simultaneously preserves the binary terms that define those categories.

Chapter Three is Gabriela Abrasowicz's "Manifestations of Transfer in the Latest Post-Yugoslav Playwriting and Theatre: Migration, Cultural Mobility and Transculturality". The basic aim of this paper is to describe specific character of dramatic works and theatrical productions about migration at the end of the twentieth and beginning of the twenty-first centuries in Bosnia and Herzegovina, Croatia, Kosovo, Macedonia, Montenegro, Serbia, and Slovenia.

Eric Trinka's "Migrants, Identity, and Body Modification in Biblical and Ancient Near Eastern Media" is Chapter Four. Trinka is concerned with the depiction of migrant acculturation in the contexts of mobility and migration in the ancient world. He demonstrates how the story of Joseph, perhaps best known in its Biblical form, as a stylized literary depiction of a forced migrant can be understood in relationship with other forms of stylized media regarding mobility, migration, and body-modification in the ancient Near East.

The second part of the book has three chapters. Chapter Five is Bianca Florentina Cheregi's 'The new diaspora' and interactive media campaigns: The case of Romanians migrating to the UK after Brexit". This chapter focuses on discourses and counter-discourses in the specific context of Romanians migrating to the United Kingdom. The analysis reveals the role of Romanian and British journalists in the problematization of migration, taking into account two different contexts: the freedom of Romanian and Bulgarian citizens to work inside the UK as citizens of EU nations starting with January 1, 2014, and the implied rejection of such migration by the British "Brexit" referendum of June 23, 2016.

Bilgen Türkay's contribution is "Social Media and ICT Use by refugees, Immigrants and NGOs: A Literature Overview". In Chapter Six, the implications of social media and information and communication technologies in the lives of refugees and migrants are analysed. Although very important, there is little information about the experiences of refugees and migrants with these technologies. In particular, it is necessary to understand how various institutions of civil society, particularly non-governmental organizations (NGOs) mobilize this technology to aid migrants. This study attempted to understand the reasons for using social media and information and communication technologies by migrants and refugees as well as the NGO usage of social media and information and communication technologies in the process of helping them.

Barış Öktem's Chapter Seven is "Reproduction Of Desire: Overuse Of Social Media Among Syrian Refugees And Its Effects On The Future Imagination". He theorizes how the reproduction of social desire occurs through social media usage among Syrian refugees. This paper offers a perspective on the interrelations between the use of SNSs among Syrian refugees for various purposes, such as navigating their migration routes and safety, and imagining the refugee camps as a temporary habitat. As refugee camps do not provide enough space or resources for many activities, most Syrian refugees spend their time online on social media platforms as Facebook, Instagram, YouTube, and WhatsApp.

Taken together, the essays of this volume outline key representational parameters of contemporary migration. As migration patterns change, the importance of continued scholarship remains critical to understand a crucial dynamic of the contemporary world.

CHAPTER 1

REPRESENTATION OF ASYLUM SEEKERS IN SCIENCE FICTION FILMS: PRAWNS IN *DISTRICT 9*

Vildan Mahmutoğlu

Introduction

One of the major challenges in the contemporary world is immigration. Every year, many people leave their country with great hopes. "Migrant" is the general name that describes those people who leave their own country for another. But in fact, they are received and processed with different names: asylum seeker, refugee or migrant. The label, by which they are described them, depends on the mode of arrival and the nature of their stay in the host country. The subject of this study is the category of asylum seeker. The difference between asylum-seekers and migrants is that the former has not yet been officially accepted by the country in which they have arrived.

This study is about the representation of asylum seekers in a science fiction film. Whilst cinema is a technical invention, the plots of films come from society's issues. At the dawn of cinema, there was no light, no editing or scenario in the films. Film shooting was realised by natural light and space, with little embellishment. When fictional narratives started taking place in the cinema, actual social matters became the subject. Together with the industrialization of cinema and the increase in the numbers of production companies, new genres appeared. Whilst these genres took time to appear in the cinema, science fiction appeared early on.

In the early years of cinema, science fiction film was a kind of genre that presented a dream world. Initially, this dream world conveyed the idea of a positive world, a utopia, but with time it became associated with the dystopia. Whilst the subjects in science fiction films are represented as far away in the future, those chosen are drawn from the issues/problems of the society of the time. Therefore, when the subjects of science fiction cinema are examined, it can give clues about the problems of the society or the World. These threats and problems are formed as "other" in the science fiction films.

This study begins with defining the features of asylum seekers and refugees. After explaining these terms, representation in science fiction film will be discussed, as mentioned above, the subjects of science fiction cinema usually reflect concerns of contemporary society. In science fiction film, there are generally aliens from beyond Earth. They are "others" and depending on the period, they are actually such as Russians, Iranians or Communists.

The main question of this study is how the migration issue, which could be said to be the greatest challenge of our day, is depicted in the recent science fiction film *District 9*. This film was chosen as the case study, because the characters and the construction of the plot are different from the other science fiction films. The questions "How the representation of asylum seekers prepared in a science fiction film? and "How is a host country represented in a science fiction film?" will be examined in this study. Also, redemption for the humanity will be analysed as well.

Definition of Asylum Seekers

The rejection of asylum seekers is not limited to today. In the past, the Jews fled from the Nazis and sought refuge in Cuba, in May 1939. Sailing from Hamburg and carrying 937 refugees, their ship was not allowed access and had to leave for Florida. Even very close to the coast, the authorities there did not allow them to go ashore. The ship was forced to return to Europe. After this return, most of the Jews face their "absolute end" (https://encyclopedia.ushmm.org/content/en/article/voyage-of-the-st-louis).

The Refugee Council states in its definition that an asylum seeker leaves the home country and that his/her application to another country has not yet been accepted. The difference between asylum seekers and the migrants is that the former do not leave their country because of economic or educational reasons https://www.refugeecouncil.org.uk/policy_research/the_truth_about_asylum). The asylum seekers have not been accepted in any countries, but after legal applications, they are called refugees (https://www.bianet.org/bianet/bianet/2953-multeci-siginmaci-gocmen-nedir).

Asylum seekers are dependent on aid and their timeline is unclear. This process of waiting for an asylum seeker depends on the host country's conditions and the laws for immigrants there. Ultimately, the country decides who the asylum seeker is and the decision depends on the policies that they have adopted (Farrier, 2011). The difficulty in this process is that many asylum seekers are viewed as a danger for the security and independence of the country. The host countries tell asylum seekers that that they have to protect their citizens first and they can provide the services to the refugees only for a limited time. The transition process for asylum to refugee status varies from country to another, but it can be longer duration in developed countries compared to developing countries.

Representation of "others" in science fiction films

What is the word "representation"? In its original Latin, it means "to make present again". During the middle ages, the word had a mystical meaning, the term being used to create a body that was not an object (Sukla, 2001). There are many myths about the monsters. Monsters were beings that did not resemble humans, e.g. in "Oedipus and the Sphinx", "Saint George and the Dragon", "Job and the Leviathan" or "Ahab and the Whale". The human being was not safe with the existence of "monster" which could be very dangerous. War has often been taken place between human beings and monsters (Kearney, 2003). Redemption is another word that is usually used in old stories. Generally, "redemption" is related to the Word "Scapegoat". Many old cultures have myths about scapegoat strangers. According to these myths, the aliens were responsible for any wrongdoing in society and they had to be isolated or destroyed for its own sake. Even though these myths were constructed in the past, today, their traces can still be seen in our lives. For example, in Greco-Roman myths, Prometheus, Dionysius and Romulus paid for the sins of the society. In the contemporary world, also, what is unfamiliar is seen as a threat and "evil". The strangers or things that are not familiar to humans are considered as enemies. "We" are the human beings and there are the "others" as enemies (Kearney, 2003). Non-humans can be seen as being responsible for human sins.

The "genre" is a French word that means "type" or "kind" (Neale, 2000). At the beginning, cheap popular novels enable the concept "genre" settle into the public. With the development of capitalism, many different genres of novels are published. They are for the "public", many people can understand them easily. Subsequently, with entrepreneurs looking for new excitement to promote to the public, the first short films were made and cinema was starting to be considered commercial. These developments allowed for the introduction of different genres in cinema (Abisel, 1995). Genre can be seen in all cultural products. Science fiction, can be found in novels, films and other cultural products (Geraghty, 2009). Science fiction is a genre but it is different from the other genres. Because they renew themselves every 10 years. Science fiction films always tell the present time problems in future time (Kolker, 2009).

There are different approaches and definitions about what science fiction cinema is. Science fiction writer Isaac Asimov said that science fiction as a branch of literature and it is the people's answer to technology and science. The characters of science fiction are unknowns, such as the nonhuman. They can be creatures, robots, spacecrafts or rockets. Even as these definitions give clues about what science fiction genre is, they don't reveal the full definition. Tzvetan Todorov stated that the best science fiction has a common structure; first of all, the subjects are supernatural. The characters are from the space or they are robots. Todorov pointed out that whilst the characters come from outside of our world, the events relate to the situations relating to that which we live in. So, the science fiction reader is kept between the existence of an unknown world and the existence of a known one (Cornea, 2007).

The definition of genre in cinema can be summarized as referring to commercial films that tell similar stories in similar conditions with similar characters. They have common features and they are produced around them. Regarding for the genre films, it can be said that since they have been tried before, there is less risk at the box office. The definition and discussion of film genres gather around mainstream- commercial films (Kabadayı, 2018). In science fiction films, "others", non-human characters, are always positioned against human beings. Aliens usually represent badness, whilst Earthmen represent goodness and at the end of the film, humanity emerges on top. Otherness is against human beings. They are "creatures" and they are used in order to display fears and worries (Cornea, 2007). In these films, strong and bad creatures appear as "masters" coming from space. These masters are either creatures or human-looking aliens trying to conquer the world (Oskay, 2014).

The subjects in movies may sometimes come from present-day problems, but sometimes they are taken from the history. It could be seen like there is nothing remain of the problems on these days, but it could continue to emerge in the works of art. The concepts developed by Hayden White and Robert Rosentsone explain how narrative issues emerged from history. "White says that narrated history should have a different kind of representing history" (Ibrahim, 2009:3). Robert Rosentone develops his idea and states that the products of these narrations are not documentary. There is another constitution of dramatic structure for them. Rosenstone says that it is telling history in a dramatic film. It is not just a documentary film; it is telling the history in a dramatic film. Rosenstone explains that some historical facts can be narrated in a dramatic film, but juts not in a documentary. Afterwards, White develops his own idea and Rosenstone's notion further and gives the concept of "historiophoty". It means, "representation of history in audio-visual media" (Ibrahim, 2009:4).

Science fiction films consist of stories edited between the known world and the unknown world. When we look at these films according to the periods, we can see how the problems of the period are made in the films.

Periods in science fiction cinema

As aforementioned, the topics of science fiction films are inspired by the society's problems and its fears. So, the analysis of science fiction films proceeds by splitting into time periods in order to enable us to understand the background to each more clearly and to establish a connection with the plots of films (Kaplan & Ünal, 2011).

Utopia in the period of silent motion pictures (1900-1929)

The first years of cinema were also the first years of science fiction cinema. In those days, the films were generally aimed at showing future events in a positive light. No wars or great destruction had yet been introduced. Hence, the public had the belief that everything in the future would be very good and a utopian perspective was dominant in the films. In those days, the notion of dystopia was absent and there was no fear generated or problems raised in the films. That is, the films had optimistic viewpoints and they drew pictures of fantastic future worlds (Çoker, 2016). Films, such as *Voyage dans la Lune* (1902), *Time Machine* (1895) are *Voyage au Centre de la Terre* (1904) are the examples of the first years of cinema. In this period, there was no dramatic structure, and the main aim was to entertain audiences by surprising them. The first science fiction film maker, Melies, was an illustrator who delivered tricks visually. When Melies' silent film *Voyage dans La Lune* was shown, the term "genre" had yet to coined.

After Melies, in 1927, in Germany, Fritz Lang produced the film *Metropolis*, which is generally accepted as the first real science fiction. It was made after the First World War and was greatly influenced by the expressionist movement. In this film, the lives of the working class and the elites are portrayed. The workers, who have to live in an underground city, are under the control of Rotwang (Kolker, 2009), who was the first mad scientist in this genre. Andrew Tudor writes that Rotwang "wanted no more than to rule to world" (Geraghty, 2009). Rotwang exemplifies the ambition of people at the moment the science fiction genre starts. Understanding that science can be also used in malevolently begins with the end of the First World War. For instance, it was acknowledged that science could be used to develop more advanced technical weapons for war. So, it could not just be used to create a utopian world, but also, a dystopian one, which was reflected in the science fiction cinema of the period and ever since.

Losing hope in Science Fiction Cinema (1930-1950)

The second period in science fiction film starts with the great depression and continues up until the end of the Second World War. The destructive power of science and technology finally kills off the optimistic atmosphere in the world.

At the start of this period, expressionism influenced science fiction cinema, as an artform, this started in Germany at the end of the nineteenth century. For expressionist artists, art breaks the rules of naturalism (Kurtz and all, 2016). In expressionist films, like with expressionist art, there was rebellion against naturalism and this was initially forcefully registered in German cinema. It was a time when science fiction cinema became a genre. Films, such as *Frankenstein* (1931), *The Island of Dr Moreau* (1932) and *Dr Jekyll and Mr. Hyde* (1931) were made. One common factor is that all these films have mad scientist character. These fiction characters first of all took place in novels. *The Island of Dr Moreau* was written in 1896 by H.G. Wells and first adapted for cinema in 1932. The film takes place on an imaginary island in the South Pacific which is controlled tyrannically by Dr Moreau. He carries out some experiments on humans and animals. Also, he implements his philosophy of creating superior posthumans. Society on the island is the first to be dominated by a mad scientist (Dinello, 2005). Another film is *Frankenstein*, written by Mary Shelley in 1818 and adapted for cinema by James Whale in 1931. Dr. Frankenstein creates a monster, through combining parts taken from corpses. Elizabeth Young states that the political metaphor included in this film can be used for analysing contemporary world problems. In other words, it refers to problems of its era. In the film, the monster fights with his creator Dr. Frankestein. The creatures that emerges in this unnatural way ends up fighting with its own creator. The monster, whilst carrying out despicable acts of violence, is also treated with some sympathy, whereas the creator is vilified for his evil use of his knowledge (Young, 2008).

There are scientists who try to control the world, and they create a dystopic atmosphere by saying that they can think best for the rest of society. The aforementioned films tell about these scientists' destructive passions. According to these mad scientists, for the good of the rest of the world, people of some subclasses or creatures must make sacrifices. After the sacrifice of others, the society can be happier.

Cold War in the science fiction cinema (1950-1970)

The Second World War ended with the atomic bomb. At the end of the war, the world is divided into two big blocks; one side is the Soviet Union and the other side is the United States. In this Cold War period of 1950-1970, a witch-hunt against communists is performed with McCarthyism whose name comes from U.S. Republican senator Joseph McCarthy. Under the McCarthy investigation of U.S. cinema, many people were arrested.

Also, another very important incident in this period is the Cuban Revolution. These two events affected U.S. society, creating a reaction from science fiction cinema (Çoker, 2016). Apart from these facts, other important things can be experienced in the society. For example, the first reported UFO was seen in 1957. Space sciences become more popular with the appearance of the first UFO (Roloff & SeeBlen, 1995).

The years between 1950 and 1970 are a turning point of the science fiction genre. The Cold War period was the golden age of science fiction cinema. The general picture of the period gives the reason for the increase in such film production (Cornea, 2007). When the films between 1950 and 1970 are examined, they provide clues about the period. Some people believe that the protection of the world against communists inside and aliens outside was conjured up by the United States, because of its power. For example, in *Destination Moon* (1950), the moon has very rich uranium deposits and the US captures it to exploit these resources, claiming it is justified in doing so. Films like this can be considered as paving the way for pursuing colonialism, as happened in Vietnam and South America (Roloff & SeeBlen, 1995). In another film, called *Project Moon base* (1953), after arriving on the Moon, one of three crew members dies. A woman commander and a male astronaut are left, who get married there. The ceremony is held for the world to see, with the traditions of human beings so the United States carries the traditions from earth to the moon. *Unknown World* (1951) is about the aftermath of a nuclear war. At the end of the war, scientists look for caves on earth that aren't affected by radiation, with the film generally being about their struggle to survive (Roloff & SeeBlen, 1995). Another film in this period is *The Red Planet Mars* (1952). In the film, Peter Graves, who is a scientist, detects radio waves coming from Mars. These messages say that God is alive and lives there. God sends messages to the earth by Morse code. When they decode the Morse code, they see that God doesn't want the Stalinist regime and communism in the Soviet Union. God doesn't want atheist people also and He wants everyone to believe in Christianity (Dixon, 84). The world was divided into two parts during this time period: communist and capitalist. So, even though the subjects in the films are the subject of science fiction, the messages are about the cold war. The "other" in these films are the Russians and the communists.

A Shining Era for Science Fiction films: The 1970 onwards

The development of technology in the United States also influenced Hollywood films. After the marketing of films, companies also sold merchandise of the characters created (Geraghty, 2009). Cinema became profitable for the economy and the US, in particular made and sold different types of films all over the world. The future was looking bright for science fiction cinema, with many important films being made after 1970. For example, *1984*, which is George Orwell's most famous book and one of the foremost dystopian works, was turned into a screenplay. The words "Big Brother" and "thought crimes" are his contributions to the dystopian world. Orwell's works are not just literary works, but also have sociological connotations (Cushman & Rodden, 2004).

Redemption has not been used much in science fiction film since the 1970s. People have been left to their own fate, that is, they have been left to overcome problems and threats themselves. If we consider the important examples of science fiction in this period, one that must not be overlooked *Star Wars* (1977). It is one of the films that uses the "other" very clearly. *Star Wars* earned over 130 million dollars in the US, heralding Hollywood's new era (Geraghty, 2009). After many dystopic alien films, friendly aliens were seen in films between 1977 and 1988. During this period, not only the relationship between aliens and adults, but also the friendships between children and aliens come to the fore. In this period, the most popular science fiction film was *E.T.* It is released in 1982. After his ship accidentally left him on Earth, E.T. finds himself in the boy Elliot's family's garden. With the help of E.T., he deals with many familial troubles. Elliot sees that the real problem is not the alien, but the narrow-mindedness of people (Geraghty, 2009).

Another science fiction film, *RoboCop* (1987), is set in Detroit, a declining Rust Belt city. Living standards have fallen, with there being high unemployment and many people have left the city to seek work elsewhere. Those who have not left are suffering from economic hardship and poverty. Omni Consumer Products (OCP), a multinational company, starts to manage the Detroit Police Department. In the film, it is mentioned that "changes in tax structures prepare an ideal environment for companies to grow, but this is at the detriment of public services." As a result of the privatisation of the police, the company, which is also a robot supplier, develops a new model of policing cyborg, half human and half robot. Severely injured, Officer Alex Murphy is transformed into Robocop. The city's situation gets worse, with crime increasing. Murphy's memory is fully robotised, but later his human memory is restored (Bould, 2015). The decline in income, the problem of unemployment and rampant technology constitute the plot of the film.

In the 2000s, *The Matrix* series was a big hit. This triology, which questions artificial intelligence and human existence problems, was made by the Wachowski Brothers. The first film of the series, released in 1999, details a war between human-looking machines with artificial intelligence and human beings. The human-looking machines program human life and this is very difficult to change. The program has been developed by the artificial intelligence as "others" (Sanders, 2008).

When all the periods are examined, it clear that society's contemporary problems are being addressed. As the main subject of this study is the reflection of social problems in science fiction cinema, the immigration problem in contemporary film will be examined. Specifically, the aim is to analyse immigration in the science fiction film *District 9*.

Method

It is generally accepted that, even when science fiction cinema says something about the future, it is actually considering a present-day concern. Content analysis is used to analyse the film. After providing a summary of the film, why the aliens are seen as asylum seekers in the film is examined. In the next section, the problems faced by asylum seekers in the presence of the host country is also analysed. The sacrifice of the "other" for humanity is considered in the final section.

District 9 was directed by Neill Blomkamp and written by Neill Blomkamp and Terri Tatchell. The producer was Peter Jackson and the film was released by TriStar Pictures on 14 August 2009. The budget was 30 million dollars, whilst it had earned more than 203,600,000 dollars worldwide by the end of November 2009. The film was nominated for four Academy Awards in 2010.

District 9 - Summary

The story takes place in Johannesburg, South Africa, in 1982. One day a huge spaceship arrives at Johannesburg and stays there for three months without any contact. After three months, special team members of the Multi-National United (MNU) enter the spaceship and they see the aliens within. They are sick and they need help. They cannot leave the city, because the propulsion system of their space ship is faulty. The aliens are called "prawns", because they appear shrimp-like to humans.

The government places the aliens in a camp and allocate their living area as under the space craft, which is called "District 9". The aliens then live in this space for 20 years without access to the outside. They are not alone in District 9, as the area attracts all kinds of illicit activities. It is a place where all kinds of gun sales and bad business happen under the control of Nigerians, who also live there. The monitoring mission of the aliens is given to the MNU. The officers who want to disperse the occupants ask the aliens to relocate from District 9 to a place far from the city called District 10. However, they do not want to abandon District 9, but the MNU assigns an employee to take them up to District 10. Wikus Van der Merwe has to go to District 9 and announce their departure. At this time, Wikus is an insensitive person, who arrives and makes his announcement without any hesitation. He has no empathy, despite the aliens having families and friends. In one of the cottages in the camp, two prawns and one child prawn have been collecting liquid in order to escape from the earth. During the notification of MNU, Wikus sprays this liquid on himself, which an alien called Christopher Johnson has accumulated for 20 years. Christopher needs that liquid for launching his space craft again. Wikus' body starts to change because of the liquid. The transformation starts from his hands and suddenly he becomes a target, because his DNA starts to change. Wikus becomes very valuable with his changing DNA. MNU wants to use the aliens' weapons, but they cannot because of the DNA mismatch and they are designed only for the use of the aliens. Wikus will also be able to use weapons with his changing DNA. The head scientist from the MNU laboratory wants to cut Wikus's body up completely and use every part. That request is accepted by his father-in-law. At MNU, he is a top executive person and he keeps this development from his daughter.

Wikus escapes from the laboratory and takes shelter in District 9, where he cooperates with Christopher. They steal the liquid from the MNU's laboratory. They need the liquid because, as soon as they obtain it, it will cure Wikus and also activate space sleep. MNU officers attack the District 9 area to destroy it and catch Wikus and Christopher. Then, the Nigerians capture Wikus, because also they need his arm to use the alien technology. Wikus stays on Earth but helps Christopher to let leave the planet. He mans the spaceship together with his son and it disappears into the sky.

In the last scene, the transformation of Wikus is completed; apparently, he is totally a "prawn". Wikus makes a flower out of metallic waste for his wife. He has sacrificed himself for Christopher and his son. Due to its illegal activities, the government closes the laboratory and launches a formal investigation of the MNU.

Analysis

Born in South Africa, as abovementioned, Neill Bloomkamp directed *District 9* and he is also one of the scriptwriters of the film.

In 1948, the National Party came to power in South Africa and took measures to protect the rights of whites living in South Africa. They separated the regions where the whites and blacks lived. However, not just black and whites were separated. All society was divided according to colour; the Whites, the Coloured, the Bantu (black Africa) and the Asians. So, Cape Town was divided into four sections. This period was called the "apartheid regime". On February 11, 1966, the District 6 area where the blacks stayed was allocated to whites by the apartheid regime. The government roughed up the Black people who did not want to leave District 6. Over 60,000 people were removed from the black zone of Cape Town. Thus, it can be seen that Bloomkamp in his film narrates the history of Cape Town, in his country of birth. As stated by Robert Rosenstone, it is possible to describe history not just as a historical documentary, but rather to translate it into a narrative with a dramatic structure. In other words, as Hayden White terms it, this film can be identified as "historiophoty", which means telling the history within the dramatic structure by audio visual technologies. This is what Bloomkamp did as a screenwriter and director. This time, however, differently from history, the same racist approach was imposed on aliens as the "other" and the Nigerians.

With this film, Africa becomes one of the science fiction's subjects. *District 9* opens as a documentary. In fact, it is mockumentary because it isn't real, just fictional things depicted as real. The main characters of this film are hyper-technologies, spacecraft, a dystopic city, and aliens. The film takes place in Johannesburg, South Africa, where racism, poverty and the inequality between White and Black people.

In the film, the racism theme is also examined through the Nigerians, who are doing nefarious deeds, with there being no good ones portrayed. They are murderers and thieves who run the gun trade. On the other hand, some White people are good, whilst others are bad and they are only ones belonging to the ruling class. There is a dystopian atmosphere right from the beginning.

The analyses are made through adopting both sociocultural and ideological approaches. The aliens are examined as being representative of asylum seekers. Johannesburg officers, MNU, people in the street, the experts and the journalists considered as the host country population.

Aliens as asylum seekers

The film starts off as a documentary, where specialists, consultations and public interviews in the streets are screened by the surveillance cameras. Using surveillance cameras resonates with the atmosphere of reality programs. These kinds of programs are called mockumentary programs. However, this beginning gives us the feeling that we are witnessing a real event.

In this genre, often there is an alien invasion of Earth, but in this film, the aliens are helpless. The foreigners in the ship coming from space can be seen as a metaphor for asylum seekers. What brings this to mind: first of all, their spaceship has broken down and they are forced to stay in Johannesburg. There is no communication between the space craft and the

MNU for three months. Then, first contact is made by the earthmen via the use of a camcorder. The footage doesn't give the audience the impression they are just watching a science fiction film, but rather, there is also the sense that the ship is full of illegal immigrants. As the security forces enter inside, there is a voiceover informing us that the aliens in the ship are ill and hungry. The audience watches the camcorder as a news camera and at the same time the voiceover gives the information as if it is a real event. It takes us from the fiction to giving the feeling of being a witness to a real life event. Then, the aliens are physically different from other examples of the genre, who are usually either robots or half-human-like machines and are invariably powerful. This time, the ship from space unintentionally deteriorated, and the aliens are weak and ill. Even though they are bigger and stronger than people, they are helpless. They look like a kind of giant shrimp, leading to the Johannesburg public calling them "prawns". One of whom later explains that "prawn" is also the name given to the aliens, because they eat rubbish.

In contrast to a known animal in the real world, the aliens reinforce the asylum-seeker connotation as unwanted beings. Johannesburg is not their city and nobody wants them to live there. They are on Earth because of the malfunctioning spaceship, so they need shelter. Clive Henderson, who is one of the specialists in the film, says "they don't have their own opinions, they don't receive orders and they aren't sociable". By stating this, he asserts a point of view about the asylum seekers that widely held in the present day. This shows that the aliens are not seen as equals, but rather, a low form of life. Wikus also displays a similar sense of "othering" when he states "This is our land". That is, this opinion refers to "we" and "other" and "others" are outsiders from beyond.

One of the biggest problems frequently mentioned in the film is the increasing population of the aliens, which reminds us of the concerns about increasing populations of migrants in the host countries. In the film, MNU tries to control of their population by destroying their eggs. The number of aliens was one million when they came, but this number subsequently increased to 1.8 million.

MNU makes the decision to settle the aliens at another location, because they want to get hold of all their weapons. This new place is 200 km outside of Johannesburg and when they are announcing the new camp, they hide their real intention of taking the guns. They explain the reason for changing their location as public security. They state that, if the people of Distrcit 9 vacate the city, it will become safer. Here, the term "historiophoty" come to mind again, for the same thing happened in the past in South Africa. On February 11, 1966, District 6, where blacks lived, was declared a region for whites, and the inhabitants were forcibly displaced. Over 60,000 people were moved and their homes destroyed. We can see similar scenes in the film in the attacks on *District 9*.

As it is indicated before, aliens in science fiction films don't have normal daily lives. Most of them are soldiers and/or they are in an organization that is very tyrannical. However, in the film, the aliens only fight is to escape from this Earth. One of the main characters of film is the alien Christopher Johnson. The relationship between Christopher and his son is identical to that between a human father and his son, which is unusual for aliens in a science fiction film.

Host country representations

In the first phase of the study, it was explained why aliens coming to Johannesburg could be considered as asylum seekers. In this part, the focus is on the representatives of Johannesburg: the MNU, the public, the scientists and why they can be seen as representatives of a host country in a present-day migration scenario.

At the beginning of the film, Wikus is in his office "Department of Alien Affairs" talking about the aliens, where he explains that his job is to "engage" them with society. After this, another specialist says that the aliens are "unhealthy and aimless". He adds that, all of the world is watching to them with curiosity. All these views were recorded with mobile cameras and the atmosphere created is as if it is real life. A black woman in the street says it's too expensive to have the aliens and she also adds that it is positive that there is no close contact with them. She says that it is very good that they live in a camp. Again, one of the people of Johannesburg said that the name of prawn was given to them, because they were the bottom layer who ate rubbish and resembled shrimps. When the interviews continue, people attribute the increasing crime to the aliens and argue that the city can no longer be trusted to manage the problem. In the face of this, the community hold them responsible for everything, again evoking the contemporary view that immigrants are a problem. These and similar words are what the host country people widely speak when referencing asylum seekers.

In general, as discussed above, the features of science fiction genre are that aliens are bad creatures who are trying to conquer the whole Earth. They are very strong and they are not emotional beings. They aren't interested in ordinary crimes, nor are they accused of simple theft. However, in the film, they do carry out petty crime. Moreover, usually in the genre, the aliens are feared by the public, but in this film, they are seen as prawns, very weak and pathetic. There main activities are trying to find food and protecting themselves from humans. An expert is asked whether he thinks the aliens will return to where they have come from or not. He says that at first, they came temporarily, but now he thinks that they will not return to space; they are permanently here. Later, another expert, with a sad expression, says that the aliens have become permanent residents. These interviews at the beginning of the film give the idea that the film is not a typical example of science fiction. The public hate them because they are miserable and destitute. These views of the public and experts resonate with many contemporary host country representatives.

When they were just stuck in the world, it was just a camp but in time it becomes militarised by the MNU, which controls everything about them. While MNU officers are announcing the displacement of the aliens, the non-governmental organisations around the camp are watching and protesting at their treatment of them. Banners are hung and demonstrations held against MNU. Again, this scene brings to mind the civil society organisations that try to help immigrants and asylum seekers today.

As mentioned before, the aliens' liquid dribbles onto Wikus' hand and he starts to change into a shrimp. Wikus, at first, refuses to accept this transformation, but doesn't know what to do. He keeps his secret, because he knows that nobody likes "others." When this transformation is found out, Wikus becomes a very important person in terms of biotechnology. That is, thanks to his changing DNA, he is able to use the aliens' guns. A scientist in the lab says that they need Wikus; he is now very valuable for them and he says that they can use all his body parts. The scientist says that many states and companies around the world want to have Wikus' corpse, being now worth billions of dollars. Hence, Wikus becomes a valuable commodity with his transformation.

When they raid the District 9, their are experiments on the aliens bodies in the laboratory. Foucault states that the body is valuable, if it is useful and subjected to the dominant power. He argues that one of the aims of nation-states is to control the population of human beings. In the film, MNU also try to keep under control the alien population. In order controlling the future generations, they destroy the aliens' eggs, which Wikus, at first, calls birth control. It is also seen in this film that the scientists use their knowledge to commit evil deeds, which is one of the important characteristics of the science fiction genre. That is, as mentioned before, scientists are set to use their knowledge with the ambition of controlling the world.

Wikus escapes from MNU and hides in District 9. After being physically "other", it is not possible for him to live with people. He is now one of those others and finds himself in the camp. Whilst he had no empathy as a human, as he starts to change physically, he begins to be an empathetic person. With this transformation, in fact, one question asked in the film is whether "humanity" has a connection with human appearance or not. As Wikus resembles to the aliens physically, he starts to resemble a "human" emotionally. At the end of the film, he sacrifices himself and he gives the liquid to Christopher and his son to let them to go back into space. He doesn't die but he knows his treatment is too late.

Apart from the asylum seekers and host country axis, another question asked in the film: what is redemption and what is sacrifice? Sometimes an individual makes the decision to sacrifice him/herself for the survival of the rest of society. Redemption is an event we can see in science fiction films, where some pay the atonement of their sins as decided by stronger beings. In the film, Wikus makes sacrifices for Christopher and his son of his own volition. Again, this raises the matter as to whether or not humanity is related to the human form or colour. When he transforms into an alien, he sacrifices himself. When he is a human being, he demanded for the redemption of others.

At the end of the film, an expert says that one day, they will return back to the earth, which implies that they are still in danger about aliens. In other words, the creatures who do not belong to our world always can appear as a threat. In the film's closing scene, the departure of the aliens with their ships is given as breaking news in the mocumentary style.

Conclusion

Science fiction is the name of a genre that has two main aspects: science and fiction. It is fiction in which science and technology are constructed. It retains the characteristics of the genre based on the terms it contains. However, its subjects come from what is seen as a problem and a threat in society. In fact, science fiction renews itself periodically with the technological developments of cinema. The first productions of cinema belong to science fiction and there was a utopian side in the films. The future was always handled optimistically during the early years. Melies produced the first examples of science fiction films with his adaptations of novels by Jules Verne and H.G. Wells. Then, in the First World War, it was seen that developing technology also meant new weapons with increased power of destruction. The idea that the future would be better owing to technology disappeared. Along with the wars and the economic crises, the utopian view changed to the dystopian viewpoint. As the problems/issues of the day in the world manifested themselves, these became reflected in science fiction films. That is, these films reflected the widely held concerns of the particular period in question. For the formation of a dramatic structure in a film, there must be two opposite sides: the protagonist and antagonist characters. For this reason, problems, threats appear as others and antagonist characters in such films, whereas human beings, in general, are protagonists who represent good.

Today, one of the biggest issues is migration and in particular, forced migration has changed the structure of societies. There are regularly new incidents between the host and home countries, both having many problems that are difficult to solve. Whilst the "other" was accorded to aliens, as is nearly always the case with this genre, for probably the first time, a weak, hungry and sick alien group was portrayed. The personification of the aliens as asylum seekers brought into the picture the reactions of the host country as represented by MNU, scientists, the public and experts. One of the biggest challenges of our age is immigration and director of the film *District 9* has used it to critique its current widely promoted narratives. He poses the question what makes us human? And answers this through his script as not being about physical appearance, but down to possessing humanistic ethics and human values.

References

Abisel, N. (1995). Popüler Sinema ve Türler, İstanbul: Alan Yayıncılık.

Agamben, G. (1998). *Homo Sacer: Sovereign Power and Bare Life* (1 edition; D. Heller-Roazen, Trans.). Stanford, Calif: Stanford University Press.

Agamben, G. (2000). *Means without End*. Retrieved from https://www.upress.umn.edu/book-

Agamben-Jones, D. (2002). Healing Internalized Racism: The Role of a Within-Group Sanctuary Among People of African Descent. *Family Process, 41*(4), 591–601. https://doi.org/10.1111/j.1545-5300.2002.00591.x

Bernhard Roloff, Georg See Blen, (1995). Ütopik Sinema, Çev: V. Atayman&Z.Atayman, İstanbul: Alan Yayıncılık.

Bould, M. (2015). Bilim Kurgu, Çev: S.Okan, E.Genç, İstanbul: Kolketif Kitap.

Cornea, C. (2007). Science Fiction Cinema: Between Fantasy and Reality, Edinburgh: Edinburgh University Press.

Coker, N.B. (2016). Bilim Kurgu Sineması 1900-1970, İstanbul: Seyyah Kitap.

Cushman, T., Rodden, J., (2004). George Orwell: Into the Twenty-First Century, London: Routledge.

Dinello, D. (2005). Technophobia! Science Fiction Visions of Posthuman Technology, Austin, TX: University of Texas Press.

Farrier, D. (2011). Postcolonial Asylum: Seeking Sanctuary before the Law, Liverpool: Liverpool University Press.

Geraghty, L. (2009). American Science Fiction Film and Television, New York: Berg.

Ibrahim, A. https://www.academia.edu/24240528/Title_of_Essay_Adapting_

Kaplan, N., Ünal, G., (2011). Bilim Kurgu Sinemasını Okumak "Göstergebilimsel Yaklaşım", İstanbul: Derin Yayınları.

Kabadayı, L. (2018). Film Eleştirisi, İstanbul: Ayrıntı Yayınları.

Kearney, R. (2003). Strangers, Gods and Monsters: Interpreting otherness, London: Routledge.

Kolker, R. (2009). Film, Biçim ve Kültür, Çev: Ertınaz ve diğerleri, Ankara: De Ki Basım Yayın.

Kurtz, R. (2016). Expressionism and Film, New Barnet: John Libbey Publication.

Neale, S. (2000). Genre and Hollywood, London: Routledge.

Oskay, Ü. (2014). Popüler Kültür Açısından Çağdaş Fantazya, Bilim-Kurgu ve Korku Sineması, İstanbul: Der Yayınları.

Sanders, S.M. (2008). The Philosophy of Science Fiction Film, Lexington: University press of Kentucky.

Sukla, A.C. (2001). Art and Representation: Contributions to Contemporary Aesthetics, Westport: Praeger.

Wilmer, S. E. (2018). Performing Statelessness in Europe. UK: Palgrave Macmillan.

Young, I. M. (2011). *Justice and the Politics of Difference* (Revised ed. edition). Princeton, N.J: Princeton University Press.

Young, E. (2008). Black Frankenstein: The Making of an American Metaphor, New York: New York University Press.

https://www.coe.int/en/web/human-rights-channel/refugees-and-migration/videos/-/asset_publisher/j61mOEdcdaWp/content/when-you-don-t-exist- When you don't exist... (2012, September 10). Retrieved September 27, 2018.

CHAPTER 2

BORDER IMAGERY AND REFUGEE ABJECTION IN CONTEMPORARY VISUAL ART

Balca Arda

Border Imagery and Refugee Abjection in Contemporary Visual Art

Long before the United Kingdom's never-ending Brexit process for leaving the European Union or Donald Trump's rule in the United States, nativism, nostalgic nationalism and the priorities of border security, together with the rejection of globalization, international institutions and alliances, have been articulated in desired migration destinations. The thematic of illegal immigration, refugee criminality and hostility to migrants, strict management of visa applications for tourists, international students or permanent card holders have become the highlights of daily public and administrative debate. As a result, borders, frontiers, walls, fences, check points, security architecture have overloaded in every day's news images while controversial changes for regulations of border management and immigration policy have been legislated. Latest examples of humanity's tragedy regarding migration management continue to be poignant, such as the April 2016 deal between the European Union (EU) and Turkey about closing borders of the Balkan migration route to the EU; the Trump administration's family separation implemented in January 2018 for illegal parent migrants who are deemed criminals and separated from their children; and finally Colombia, Ecuador, and Peru recently started to ask for passports at border control for Venezuelan migrants (Matamoros, 2018).

As restrictive border management and isolation policies expanded, so did the art production about migration. Besides the overload of border imagery (e.g., masses of refugees eager to illegal entry), and the security discourse, contemporary artists engage, too, with the nowadays overgrowing materiality and visibility of political isolationism, and anti-migrant attitudes. These artistic manifestations aim to reframe the fantasy of border, belonging, and the self to search for reconciliation between host communities and newcomers. For sure, art that focuses on the cross-border is not new considering the spectacular cultural production about the Mexico/U.S.

borderlands such as the works of the famous BAW/TAF, San Diego-based Border Arts Workshop. Yet, migration crises at global scale in recent years have provoked a global, and hence new, artistic upsurge. Reinserted concept of "interior frontiers" by Etienne Balibar (Balibar & Williams, 2002: 76) indicates the subjective internalization of the idea of the border and the moral barricade against erosion of the nation and the self (Stoler, 2017) by tracing impenetrable borders between groups. As such, tactics of art display follow the fact that imagination of territory surpasses geographic understanding and extends to the contours of the self. Thus, "frontier" defines the affective contours of a protective and precarious threshold of belonging and not belonging (Stoler, 2017).

This chapter explores this accelerating artistic production on the border imagery and its relation to abjection, how contemporary art aims to interrupt refugee abjection and what are the limits of such an artistic endeavour. To be sure, the border imagery connotates the thematic of the body and its suffering. This perspective deliberately brings to mind the concept of "abject" together with the representation of the migrant and precisely refugee in a variety of artistic practices. According to Julia Kristeva, the operation "to abject" is fundamental to the maintenance of the subject and the society, while the condition of "to be abject" is subversive of both formations (Foster, 2015: 16). Thus, "locking oneself up allows one to prove one's own existence as well as the fact that his/her community can last along" (Szary, 2012: 219), while migrants transgress the membrane of the host society's way of being.

Anti-migrant sentiment and discourse, such as interior borders built against migrants (Balibar & Williams, 2002), represent the abject figuration of migrants who supposedly "aimed to disturb the given orderings of subject and society alike" (Kristeva, 1982: 2). The abject "incites fear and loathing because it exposes the border between self and other as constructed and hence fragile, and thereby threatens to dissolve the subject by dissolving the border" (Young, 2011: 144). The abject disturbs boundaries, for instance, between the living and the dead, human and animal, human and alien, male and female while the migrant assumed to be abject break the frontiers of citizen and non-citizen. Kristeva defines abject as a category of (non)-being (Kristeva, 1982) and what a subject must get rid of to become a subject at all. Therefore, the abjected as impure is constructed as "deviating from an essential state of originary homogeneity" (Duschinsky, 2013: 711). "Dirt, vomit, skin parts and alike examples of the abjected are always both alien to the subject and intimate with it, thereby this over-proximity produces a panic in the subject" (Foster, 2015: 14). This implies that the abject verges on the fragility of the boundaries of the self and hence distinction between our insides and outsides. Indeed, migration of people for better opportunities of jobs, education and quality of life as well as because of mass displacement due to conflicts, massive violations of human rights or socio-economic disturbance challenge national subject and nation-state sovereignty. The border separates "embarrassing images of chaos" hence "abjective" fluidity and "comforting images of order" (Brown, 2010: 92). Thus, the essential function of the border and its circulating imagery is to assist materializing and imagining territoriality and its legitimacy. The refugee, "by breaking the identity between the human and the citizen and between nativity and nationality, brings the originary fiction of sovereignty to crisis" (Agamben, 2000: 21). For Judith Butler, what constitutes through division the "inner" and "outer" worlds of the subject is a border and boundary tenuously maintained for the purposes of social regulation and control (Butler, 1999: 170).

As such, abjection is disciplinary through border regime that administers order via seizure in space. Refugee abjection refers to Foucault's "biopolitics" (Foucault, 1995) by reducing risks for the efficient working of the national population through the circulation of capital and of life itself. Thereby, the "citizen would be corrected and his welfare guaranteed, but the alien would be subject to forcible circulation and expulsion" (Blue, 2015: 268). Thus, abject figuration of refugee status foretells somehow the political, social and economic epidemic that the refugee can contaminate the host country. The strict discourse that projects refugees and illegal migrants as economically superfluous, or biologically or politically dangerous to the national health and body, essentially derives from the underneath sense that border management is for "walling out more poor from less poor parts of the world" (Brown, 2010: 113), or "hidden apartheid concerns the populations of the 'South' as well as the 'East'" (Balibar & Williams, 2002: 76). Eventually, if we undertake the abject horror of the refugee camp, this is not only the banalization of life through stripping away of political community hence to produce *bare life*, a life beyond political and legal representation as it is in Agamben's perspective (Downey, 2009). But more importantly, refugee abjection has also been textualized with an image of *bare life* without means of subsistence or possibility of welfare. This coincides with refugee's assumed economic dependence and unproductiveness for the given host community, under which the refugee signs in. Therefore, anti-migrant attitudes generally support the argument that refugee is not someone acting on the right of necessity; and that most of the economic migrants pretending to be refugees, while claiming that refugees cross borders not only to save their lives but also to get a share from the prosperity enjoyed in the host community.

For sure, the corporeality of refugee's media representations that mostly emphasizes on the visual suffering of migrant's isolated body lead the social stigmatization of newcomers as unable, degenerative, and superfluous, triggering debates about risks of receiving such migration that threatens the "healthy" state of the nation. Undoubtedly, this implies ableism as criteria regarding the merit of migration. As Campbell notes, ableism produces a particular kind of self and body as "the corporeal standard that is projected as the perfect, species-typical and therefore essential and fully human while disabled one is seen as diminished state of being human" (Campbell, 2009, 44). Thereby, ableism presents a subjecthood versus the abjection notion consists of discourses and structures that have created a process and system by which people have been banned based on real and perceived mental and physical disabilities, as well as for prevailing notions of inferiority, deviancy, threat, and unproductivity (Sekerci & Altiraifi, 2018). As such, the subjecthood is granted to the ideal in a capitalist knowledge based society that values productivity (Niles, 2018) while discriminated and stigmatized groups and individuals even without physical disability need to "prove" their ability to produce. As a matter of fact, the humanitarian refugee acquisition that favours ethical rather than material concerns challenge ableist ideals of citizenship that sign up for communal belonging.

Yet, contemporary art is well-known for engaging with ethics as humanitarian cause predicts. Such ethical engagement of contemporary art can follow a very specific thematic of politics, which focuses on the spectacle of suffering to activate public discourses and political act. In that sense, such works of contemporary art may intend to give voice to the oppressed or reveal what is concealed in the reality of the social (Rancière, 2011). To arouse pity, suffering and wretched bodies must be conveyed in such a way to affect the sensibility of those who are more fortunate. Therefore, the mission of contemporary art becomes to create ways of sensibility to evoke pity. For some cases, contemporary art cannot totally differ from the corporeal rapprochement of mass media to portray numerous global misfortunes, including mass migration encapsulated within border management. This spectacle aims to provide contact between these two classes for those who are fortunate to be able to observe, either directly or indirectly, the misery of the unfortunate. Hannah Arendt argued that the "politics of pity" is distinguished from the "politics of justice" that is based directly on action, on the order of merit; rather, the former is just about the observation of the unfortunate by those who do not share their suffering (Arendt, 2006: 59–114). According to Arendt's analysis, the opposition between compassion and pity is as the following: "Compassion is linked to the presence and thereby apparently local whereas pity generalizes and integrates the dimension of distance" (Boltanski, 1999: 6). From this angle, humanitarian politics that employs politics of pity holds the boundary between the fortunate and the unfortunate. That is because compassion necessitates politics of justice that demands action with reference to communal merit instead of chance and coincidence.

I contend that contemporary art on refugee abjection must be studied through the contextualization of the politics of pity versus the politics of justice to better understand the potentiality of these artistic practices to reach anti-migrant sensibilities deriving from the notion of ableism for citizenship. Studying these artistic practices through theoretical terminology permits to question how representative practices themselves have come to form and aim to transform political practices, as in this case of border policy debates. The prominent role of border priority in its theories and practices on abjection make contemporary art that is related to this topic a decisive field of inquiry to conceptualize terms of artistic reconciliation and oppositional trends against otherization while popularization of isolationism prevails at global level. Such an examination allows to think about how difference is produced and generated, as well as what kinds of representational projection can reconcile the conflicts of interests between various publics that constitutes the society including host and incoming members. Contemporary art as site of signified and signifying achieves an alternative arena of public discussions. As Rancière claims, contemporary political art firstly works like "a mini-demonstration of testimony for democracy or co-presence to repair the lost social bonds of the community" (Rancière, 2009). Artistic practices that resist refugee abjection reveal deadlocks at the time when there is an accelerating decline in popular trust for elite rule to remedy accelerating inequalities in the socio-political and especially economic system.

In the following part, I will explore some of the artistic practices resisting refugee abjection. These artworks aim to reverse the abjective perception of migrants as "worthless" and "harmful" according to the ableist context, in order to reconcile host community and newcomers and disrupt interior frontiers, challenge xenophobic political discourses, and delegitimize restrictive policies of border. While numerous artistic practices by and about refugees tend to intervene in the political arena to offer creative insight, not every creative intervention proposes a make-over story to resituate the refugee versus citizen paradigm. As S.E.Wilmer surveyed in contemporary art, identification of refugees with characters of Greek tragedy in contemporary adaptations and other creative involvements that exhibit ideal examples of solidarity with refugees in addition to the records of actual events relying mainly on interviews with individual refugees address matters related to social justice and aim to raise awareness (Wilmer, 2018). This kind of validation of refugee journey and appreciation of hospitality in these artistic works definitely resist refugee abjection through either equalizing ethical behavior to solidarity with displaced newcomers or granting subjecthood to refugee rather than displaying sufferings of statelessness as a matter of pity. However, the artworks mentioned in the next section configure ways of remedying the abject content by imagining citizens as refugees and refugees as citizens while they also encompass a sense of similar border prescription whereas such makeover story between the refugee and the ideal citizen is assumed to ease interior frontiers between host and incoming members of society. I claim that this art maneuver precisely delivers the essential correctives in reframing anti-migrant sensibilities and in reaching diverse host publics.

Working of Contemporary Art on Refugee Abjection

Once abject art used to celebrate drawing the spectacle to the place where meaning collapses as a way of deconstructing the already given precepts and hierarchies of social order. "Abject matter expelled from the body's insides such as blood, pus, sweat, excrement, urine, vomit, menstrual fluid, and the smells were often used to express necessary testimonials against power and to witness to a special truth residing in abject states, in damaged bodies" (Foster, 2015: 27). Yet, abjection and abject representation for disadvantageous groups provokes inverse effect; thus, refugees are considered as already lacking the means of societal order and as seeking a state's protection. As a matter of fact, the refugee abjection does not emancipate either "the one that abjects" or "the one who is abjected" because it does not activate agency for self-improvement but rather fortification of the boundary between the citizen and the migrant. To challenge this effect, artists attempt to make the audience think otherwise, and activate empathy in order to nullify otherization. For this, these artworks depict imaginary or factual makeover for the citizens to think themselves in the place of refugee situation. Such art practices certainly indicate communal assumptions of what kind of self and belonging the citizenship traits consist of as well as what is not included within its borders.

Abdalla Al Omari's artwork *the Vulnerability Series* (2017), composed of large volume oil/mixed media on canvas paintings in addition to a short film, present the world leaders such as Donald Trump, Vladimir Putin, Kim Jong-un and more, as refugees themselves, imagining them under rough life conditions that actual refugees assumed to face daily. For instance, in these paintings, Putin is portrayed as a homeless, Assad appears helpless and doused in water wearing only an origami boat on his head, Trump is depicted as a refugee holding a child and his family picture in his hand, while the painting "The Queue" pictures an endless food line of people including Israeli Prime Minister Netanyahu, Iran's President Rouhani and former U.S. President Obama, all carrying empty tableware. *The Vulnerability Series* was exhibited at Ayyam Gallery (22 May-1 July 2017) in Dubai and Affenfaust Galerie (30 June–8 July 2017) in Hamburg. This artwork has been discussed in various mass media art news such as Figaro (Romanacce, 2017), the *Washington Post* (Philips, 2017) and CNN Style (Qiblawi, 2017). Al Omari, an artist and Syrian refugee settled in Belgium, states that he aimed to send an urgent message to the world leaders that likely seem to be indifferent to the humanity's crisis. The artist mentions in his artist website:

Intimate hours I spent with them have thought me more than I could imagine. Just as easily as everything worth defending can become defenseless, moments of absolute powerlessness can give you superpowers. Even I felt sorry for (my version of) Assad. In this universe without gravity, all we can hold on to is our vulnerability. I have convinced myself it is the strongest weapon humankind possesses, way more powerful than the trail of power games, bomb craters and bullet holes in our collective memories. Vulnerability is a gift we should all celebrate ('The Vulnerability Series', n.d.).

Omari also claimed that his intention was not to disrespect world leaders, but to "give them back their humanity" (Qiblawi, 2017): "Somehow my aim shifted from an expression of anger that I had... to a more vivid desire to disarm my figures, to picture them outside their positions of power." In addition to this, the artist also argues that the media depicts refugees without personalizing stories and there is chance of connecting to those people on a personal basic level with individualized stories (Ruechert, 2017).

For sure, Omari attempts to flip the narrative on power and privilege through *The Vulnerability Series,* illustrating a make-over art piece that transform statesman to man without state and hence without property. Although Omari claims that these figures of political leadership achieve the real power of humanity through this imagined transformation to vulnerable refugees, headlines on the artwork series interpret his artistic gesture to be an act of "sweet revenge" (Philips, 2017; 'Sweet Revenge', n.d.). That is because figures of subject position that nations and nation-states are identified with become abject while they are pictured as lining up for food. Such artistic initiative contradicts the fact that these political celebrities are subject to their clearly owned and hence individualized faces and recognizable names with them in these paintings. That is because the distinction between refugee and political leaders is the highest range in the sense of as such Aristotelian definition of the polis builds on the opposition between "life" as bare life and "good life" as the political (Agamben, 1998: 2–3): "There is politics because man is the living being, who, in language separates and opposes himself to his own bare life (Agamben, 1998, 8)".

Thus, as Giorgio Agamben asserted, politics signifies the passage of the voice aka *phoné* meaning sign of pain and pleasure to language, which is logos that manifests the fitting and unfitting of the just and unjust (Agamben, 1998: 7). Accordingly, political leaders' makeover of refugee status suggests the unification of two distinct spheres that commonly entails birth of politics in liberal social contract theories in the sense of the passage from the state of nature to society. The artist's statement accentuates that he favours the power of humanity against political power that cannot accomplish the settlement of justice, although it encompasses this task. Thereby humans who control state power of high degree are counterbalanced by humans only with sheer power of humanity that is not corrupted by the absolute power of politics. Here sheer power of humanity consists of the survival in the middle of unfortunate events without having any life and security guarantor such as the state and society. Thus, *bare life* that is believed to activate inferior capacity of human flourishment and part of animalistic instinct in fact enhances human power. As Kristeva notes, "by way of abjection, primitive societies have marked out a precise area of their culture in order to remove it from the threatening world of animals or animalism, which were imagined as representatives of sex and murder" (Kristeva, 1982: 12–13). This implies that those fragile states that commonly marked with abjection" (Kristeva, 1982: 12) must be embraced in order to build our essential human subjecthood.

Yet, the *Vulnerability Series* is perceived as a fantasy work and not a representation of humanity's power. The "revenge" fantasy assumed that artwork replaces masses without IDs, and any individualized trait with political leaders, so that viewers can easily recognize them at first look. Hence, artistic justice offered by a refugee artist's hand commands that these statesmen of political power encounter *bare life* conditions, whether in refugee or homeless status. That is because these portrayed figures cannot empathize with the abjected people and provoke these kinds of humanity's crisis while they command the regulation of strict border management. Such artistic justice proposal indeed presumes a tragic end for statesmen in the way in which they are considered to be powerless as well as needy, and thereby avoided, rejected, and underestimated. For sure, such end can only be perceived tragic especially for statesmen, while the life conditions of refugees, homeless people, and other abject disadvantaged communities seem to be understood to be natural and deserved.

Thus, refugee's abject status does not necessarily reflect a question of misfortune versus fortune in the sense that these statesmen would never be in *bare life* position. As Iris Young inserted, "traditional politics that excludes or devalues some persons on account of their group attributes assumes an essentialist meaning of difference; it defines groups as having different natures" (Young, 2011: 157). As a matter of fact, "business-as-usual" form of ableism conjugates with internalized racism that "Critical Race Theory considers as non-aberrant but rather as a natural part of Western life" (Campbell, 2009: 17). Such ableist politics of difference based on the claim of merit does not correspond to the scholarly critique, which prevails that international migration within and from the Global South has been or is the result of unequal distribution of economic resources and of the broader postcolonial power relations on a global scale. From the angle of the ableist politics, the reason why extreme poverty is rare in the Global North and protection of one's human rights is relatively secured in the Western societies is the fair result of merit and superior human performance, whether by agency, labor or use of cunning. Such argument corresponds to an ethos of compulsory abled-bodiedness as "showcase[d] for able-bodied performance' pursuant to the incessant consuming of objects of health, beauty, strength and capability" (Campbell, 2009; McRuer, 2002). Indeed, both Western and Eastern political leaders of high statesmanship cannot be considered as just in supposedly universal moral matters, but they are assumed to be just for their own goodness or rather, more possibly, for the common good of the political community as Machiavellian realpolitik commands. As such, in the context of ableism, shamefulness is magnified in culture where the rhetoric of being a survivor, a non-victim, is powerful, and being a victim is to be "passive or deficient" (Watts-Jones, 2002). This argument in its logic follows that refugees crossing the borders unjustly violate the laws defined by the rules of international system in a way that they cannot contest (Blunt, 2018). That is why the *Vulnerability Series* that depicts the abject positioning of political leaders is perceived as imaginary and not representational, because these political leaders certainly seem to display high capacity of subjecthood in the common sense. Thereby, the "border" still exists in this artwork between the refugee and the subject of "well-deserved" citizenship.

Another artwork, *When You Don't Exist* (2012), displays another similar makeover story to remedy the interior frontiers between refugees and host communities. *When You Don't Exist* is a two-minute short video, which is a part of Amnesty International's 'When you don't exist' campaign that focuses on holding European governments accountable for their treatment of migrants at the EU's external borders. In this short film, the audience encounter an alternative reality in which migration flows become reversed, as if some violent unrests cause people to flee from Europe in mass and reach to an African country for their security. The refugee's voiceover refrains in the video as the following: "It was bad at home; we had to leave"; "dad couldn't come; I don't know where he is now" ("Amnesty International Campaign Replaces Black Immigrants With White Actors In Controversial Video," 2013). Then these imagined European refugees are forcibly taken by authorities and jailed in refugee camps (Roch, 2016). From the start of the artwork, the viewer cannot notice that these refugees are European as the video shows masses of people walking to the borders under blankets. The shocking twist of the movie reveals refugees' European IDs, when border control officers capture them. At this part, the camera focuses on the Caucasian traits of refugees with colored eyes, light skin and hair color. In the detention centre, the European refugee boy approaches to the fence in order to communicate with the African girl citizen who is playing outside; however, he could not get back a friendly response. Amnesty International states that this short video "uses powerful imagery to challenge our perspective on the human reality of experiences of migration, and make us more aware of the situation that many migrants and refugees face when trying to reach European borders" (Tena, 2015).

The film intends to make the audience see the refugee journey through the eyes of those who had to cross continents to find safety and seek asylum in other words "to put the viewer 'in the shoes' of the refugee" (Warren, 2013). Amnesty International website states that this movie displays what it feels like to be a migrant running away from a war zone in the Middle East or a poverty-stricken country in Africa ("When you don't exist...," 2012). For this, *When You Don't Exist* reverses traditional racial roles assigned according to the historical global power hierarchies. Yet, comments on the video at the Youtube channel, as it is stated in the Huffington Post, address that the problem with anti-refugee sentiments is not about racial stigmatization, and even if it were, watching this movie would not reverse but even reproduce perceived racial hierarchies: "*The truth is, this is a HUMAN on HUMAN problem, not a black/white problem*," and as another user wrote, "I guess it's 'provocative' but if people lack basic compassion to sympathize with brown refugees in the first place, I feel like we have a bigger problem here ("Amnesty International Campaign Replaces Black Immigrants With White Actors In Controversial Video," 2013)".

Undoubtedly, Amnesty video *When You Don't Exist* aims to challenge refugee stigmatization of abjection and intend to assert that it is a matter of coincidence and luck of the Western people to be wealthy and to live in desired migration destinations. Because of the focus on racial/ethnic bodily traits of the actors, such makeover story about exchanging identity roles also implies that anti-refugee attitudes possess a close relationship to the underneath racism presuming refugee status to be akin to specific ethnicities, communities, and parts of the world. Indeed, it is not directly connected to racial/ethnic differences but refugee abjection is attached to ableism that assigns no value for despised groups for ability won by merit. Thus, such make-over of white Europeans into refugees as the video portrays is a surprise for the audience, and hence, not likely to happen, in today's postcolonial, hierarchical power regime in the world. Yet, *When You Don't Exist* aims to make refugee's suffering felt by the fortunate citizens through the destruction of the border between them. In fact, the artwork presumes that the reconciliation between host and incoming communities would not happen unless the division of fixed fortunes and misfortunes is not removed. Thereby, the video both dissolves and applies the precepts of politics of pity only to make the audience observe the suffering at first hand in order to exalt pity through empathy for the abjected. However, the *Vulnerability Series* artwork does not entirely engage with the public discussions on migration acquisition based on ableism. The disputes on the "politics of justice" including perspectives of ableism is called upon to "settle concern precisely whether the ranking of people in terms of size and worth is just" (Boltanski, 1999: 4). But Amnesty video *When You Don't Exist* intends to settle concern on people in terms of the need and the coincidence of being fortunate or not.

Figure 1 Video caption, When You Don't Exist, Amnesty Campaign

In this context, the question of a possibility for critical art practice in accordance with politics of justice and not of pity can help pro-migrant groups and individuals to enroll in public debate on migration policy. Thus, as Boltanski (1999) puts it, the politics of justice necessitates the settlement of disputes by bringing the convention of equivalence to bear in a test:

> *It is only at the outcome of the test, in the course of which the conflicting parties are induced to cite the objects and aims of a shared world, that their state of 'greatness' is revealed. It is because their claims are confronted with reality that the order brought to light by the test (which a different test could challenge) can be qualified as just (Boltanski, 1999: 4).*

Thereby, action- based "politics of justice" consists in the successful restoration of harmony by arriving at fair outcomes to disputes based upon a theory of justice which takes into account a common understanding of fairness defining and evaluating the respective merits of citizens (Boltanski, 1999: 3–4). However, in the case of ableism, the abject position of refugees is already be naturalized, and hence, not disputable. Therefore, contemporary art that serves for the politics of justice must expose the inherent and historical causes of the mass emigration and criticize the historical exploitation of colonialism and imperialism as well as contemporary effects of neoliberal capitalism that increase economic and social inequalities in terms of sharing global resources and wealth, produce global imbalances, and destabilize politics and economies of developing countries. That is to say, the reason why an African citizen of colour is more likely to be a refugee than a "white" Westerner, is not about being unfortunate and born in the wrong part of the world as *When You Don't Exist* asserts, but rather the result of the historical damages that colonialism, and corporate neoliberal capitalism cause in the Global South. The perspective of politics of justice suggests that a more historically and politically informed critical approach in contemporary art is needed to support the pro-migrant cause if the artistic intention is to remedy refugee abjection.

Still, the Steve Jobs mural by Banksy has taken in charge of the politics of justice rather than politics of pity to resist refugee abjection. The Steve Jobs mural is a graffiti painting on the wall of Calais refugee camp, where thousands of migrants hoping to make it to Britain from France. Banksy's artwork, one of a series of his works in response to the refugee crisis, depicts late Apple founder's background as son of a Syrian migrant carrying an early Macintosh computer and a black trash bag with his belongings over his shoulder.

Figure 2. Photo of Steve Jobs mural by Banksy, the artist

Jobs' father was from the Syrian city of Homs but emigrated to the United States (Mulholland, 2016) after the Second World War (Kordic, 2015). Later on, the artwork has been damaged, someone added the words "London Calling" in giant letters over the top of the artwork and others smashed the protective glass case placed on the work by local authorities hoping to preserve it (Mulholland, 2016). As it was mentioned in the *Guardian* newspaper, Banksy said:

We're often led to believe migration is a drain on the country's resources, but Steve Jobs was the son of a Syrian migrant. Apple is the world's most profitable company, it pays over $7bn (£4.6bn) a year in taxes – and it only exists because they allowed in a young man from Homs (Ellis-Petersen, 2015).

The Steve Jobs mural artwork is parts of series of other works, including a version of Theodore Gericault's famous painting *Raft on the Medusa* contrasting a luxury yacht with a boat full of refugees with caption "we're not all in the same boat", which can be found at the artist's website, as well as an image of a child holding a telescope with a vulture standing on top of it (Kordic, 2015). Among all those, the critics particularly criticize Banksy's artwork of Steve Jobs as a refugee. Critics point out that although Banksy's artwork is poignant for his purpose of calling "attention to the deplorable conditions in ever-growing refugee camps around the world" (Lapowsky, 2015), migration destination countries and host communities should open their doors to refugees not just because some of them could be the next Steve Jobs, but because their lives are in danger and they urgently need help.

In fact, Banksy's Steve Jobs artwork focuses on a very essential thought, that can be widely encountered in anti-refugee discourses, which claims that refugees are an economic burden and stigmatize refugees as parasites who are not contributing, but just exploiting resources of wealthy host countries. While Banksy has been glorified to touch on the question of economic burden, many critics claim that ethical concerns rather than economic concerns must matter for host communities while assessing the situation of the refugees, since not everyone can be a Steve Jobs, but every human being deserves to live in peace. The fantasy of a border between "'us here/them there' rooted in national belonging and state identity" (Brown, 2010, 86) and derives from the competition for leftover welfare functions of the state. The citizen's once guaranteed welfare has already been not so secure following the austerity measures that implement public cuts since the 2008 economic downturn. Such risks of citizen's vulnerability conjugates with the *bare life* perception of refugees as abject without means of subsistence and productive functions for the host community. In that sense, the anti-migrant attitude derives from both differentiation from and identification with "foreigners" and is related to the anxiety about the fact that state's own citizens, especially lowest income earners, share/believe to share at some level the vulnerability of the refugees while they do not assume to merit such abject situation. Thus, abject's over-proximity to the subject provokes horror as a consequence of concern with the instability of boundaries.

As such, antipathy toward immigrants is spreading through the perception that they are not able to produce and hence not contributing to the host community. From this angle, Banksy tries to show otherwise by Steve Jobs depiction. The images of refugees arriving to Greek islands in shabby, worn-out, ragged form like the walking dead, who are incomplete, certainly raise issues of the lines between life and death. Thus, Steve Jobs artwork at Calais refugee camp depicts a refugee's son as a subject who makes profit, accelerates U.S. investment and job creation through the foundation of the Apple company, which pays taxes to the state. Such portrayal for sure contrasts the typical abjective perception of refugees as poor and desperate in terms of sustaining their lives. According to Immigration and Redistribution research conducted in six countries indicate that information on the 'hard work'" of immigrants generates more support for redistribution as long as respondents are not prompted to think in detail about immigrants' characteristics in accordance of an internalized racism (Alesina, Miano, & Stantcheva, 2018).

For sure, press images of Justin Trudeau welcoming Syrian refugees and offering new winter coats and clean toys at a Canadian airport displays the respect-merit of newcomers right now under the security of the state. Such videos of refugee stories settling in a Western wealthy country seems to generally follow the same storyline of biopolitical make-over such as the news of the *Guardian* newspaper website publishes "The story of a Somali refugee: 'Now that I'm in Sweden I feel free and very happy.'" Omar, a Somali refugee is met at Stockholm airport by the Swedish migration board, visits a doctor, gets his "right to remain" signed and learns what margarine is" (Francis & Silver, 2012). Yet, such kind of make-over stories of refugees becoming like citizens do not necessarily make these migrants subjects. Iris Young inserts that otherized groups of stigma need to "prove" through their professional comportment that they are respectable, and their lives are constantly dogged by such trials more frequently and regularly than white men (Young, 2011: 141). Still, as a matter of being chained to their bodily being which also comprise gestures, comportment and primarily language ability and accent correctness, abject Others, including refugees, cannot be "fully and un-self-consciously respectable and professional, and they are not so considered" (Young, 2011: 142). Abjection through ableism remains as a matter of host community's security of identity and subject position.

Mr. Jobs signifies what the United States stands for in a sense of economic success, profit drive, and technological advancement. As Ethan Blue indicated, "United States became a material indicator of extended life opportunities, while expulsion became a process not exactly of death, but at least, in a sense, of banishment from the elect (Blue, 2015: 268)". Thus, the artwork suggests that the next Steve Jobs now is abjected as a refugee can there be waiting for migration at "jungle" Calais refugee camp and if rejected, in fact, prospective host community risks to be abjected through losing wealth. In order to protect and sustain the U.S. way of life and ranking in the world that results in the United States being one of the most desired migration destinations, economically rational citizens are expected to react against isolationist policies. "Steve Jobs," in this context, merits to be elected for citizenship. As such, Banksy neither intends to change the traits of abjection nor question the terms of respectability and so forth. Through looking at this artwork, his target audience is expected to recognize that their welfare calculation regarding refugee acquisition can be misleading.

Conclusion: Question of Art on Politics

The traditional populist critiques against elites including the artists and the assumed cooperation of liberal values with marginalized ethnic, racial groups, and minorities can only be explored and surpassed through understanding of the conditions and terms of public debate between the polarized segments of the societies. Taking account of interior frontiers between the abjected refugee and the subjected citizen, the contemporary art that resists to refugee abjection is expected to incite political discussions to undertake considerations of justice while testimony of suffering as a spectacle to arouse pity does not correspond the current question of anti-migrant attitudes. Thus, makeover imagination of the refugee to citizen and vice versa in these artistic practices most generally undertake the division of abject versus subject position as a matter of fortune as a commonsensical method that disregards questioning the assumed terms of citizenship on merit through ableist discourse.

While an alternative artistic endeavour on the terms of politics of justice can benefit the public discussions, it risks generating ableist criteria through legitimizing the requirement of "proof" for productiveness only for already perceived degenerative communities, including refugees unless it consists of a historical analysis of hierarchical world system. Hence only the "extraordinary" Other is the "Abled" (Campbell, 2009, 3). In this situation, those in the despised groups, who unlikely will be the next Mr. Jobs, threaten to cross over the border of the subject's citizen while they are criticized for receiving social and economic benefits unfairly from the taxes paid by the citizens of the host countries. Such assumption would basically generate an ableist discourse of white supremacy that does not take into account the historical misconduct and unfairness of imperialist past and present as well as the merit of Global South's labor in creating Western wealth. In that sense, the Steve Jobs mural can support the strictly selective border management that only gives way to extraordinary Other "Abled." Thus, although such artistic aim encompasses ethical politics rather than aesthetic intention, it differs from pity driven art in the sense of favoring to construct a shared political realm for hosts and immigrant communities.

Given the wide-scale neglect of pity-oriented narrative on refugees in contemporary art, in critical artistic practices only a focus on historical and contemporary discriminations instead of fortune or misfortune, can help to open up public discussions on migration policy and remedy refugee abjection. Indeed, the politics of justice rather than the politics of pity can shift the politics of border priority. That is to say, if contemporary critical art works intend to eliminate the border between the citizen and the refugee, they need to focus not on the affection of those who are assumed to be more fortunate but on the basic human rights and historical responsibilities regarding the supposedly abject migrant. An artwork on migration and refugees can be deemed critical not when it passively expects empathy from the citizens of the developed countries but when it seeks for justice by actively disclosing the fact that the wealth, prosperity ,and privileges enjoyed by citizens of migration destinations are directly related to the historical harms and present exploitation experienced by the people who are forced to leave their countries as refugees.

References

Agamben, G. (1998). *Homo Sacer: Sovereign Power and Bare Life* (1 edition; D. Heller-Roazen, Trans.). Stanford, Calif: Stanford University Press.

Agamben, G. (2000). *Means without End*. Retrieved from https://www.upress.umn.edu/book-division/books/means-without-end

Alesina, A., Miano, A., & Stantcheva, S. (2018). *Immigration and Redistribution* (No. w24733). https://doi.org/10.3386/w24733

Amnesty International Campaign Replaces Black Immigrants With White Actors In Controversial Video. (2013, June 19). *Huffington Post*. Retrieved from https://www.huffingtonpost.com/2013/06/19/amnesty-international-immrants-black-white_n_3462275.html

Arendt, H. (2006). *On Revolution*. New York: Penguin Classics.

Balibar, E., & Williams, E. M. (2002). World Borders, Political Borders. *PMLA, 117*(1,), 71–78.

Blue, E. (2015). National Vitality, Migrant Abjection, and Coercive Mobility: The Biopolitical History of American Deportation. *Leonardo, 48*(3), 268–269.

Blunt, G. D. (2018). Illegal Immigration as Resistance to Global Poverty. *Raisons Politiques, 69*(1), 83. https://doi.org/10.3917/rai.069.0083

Boltanski, L. (1999). *Distant Suffering: Morality, Media and Politics*. Cambridge University Press.

Brown, W. (2010). *Walled States, Waning Sovereignty*. New York : Cambridge, Mass: Zone Books.

Butler, J. (1999). *Gender trouble: feminism and the subversion of identity*. New York: Routledge.

Campbell, F. K. (2009). *Contours of Ableism: The Production of Disability and Abledness* (2009 edition). New York: Palgrave Macmillan.

Downey, A. (2009). Zones of Indistinction Giorgio Agamben's 'Bare Life' and the Politics of Aesthetics. *Third Text, 23*(2), 109–125.

Duschinsky, R. (2013). Abjection and Self-Identity: Towards a Revised Account of Purity and Impurity. *The Sociological Review, 61*(4), 709–727. https://doi.org/10.1111/1467-954X.12081

Ellis-Petersen, H. (2015, December 11). Banksy uses Steve Jobs artwork to highlight refugee crisis. *The Guardian*. Retrieved from https://www.theguardian.com/artanddesign/2015/dec/11/banksy-uses-steve-jobs-artwork-to-highlight-refugee-crisis

Foster, H. (2015). *Bad New Days: Art, Criticism, Emergency*. London ; New York: Verso.

Foucault, M. (1995). *Discipline & Punish: The Birth of the Prison* (REP edition). New York: Vintage.

Francis, N., & Silver, M. (2012, August 16). The story of a Somali refugee: "Now that I'm in Sweden I feel free and very happy" – video. *The Guardian*. Retrieved from https://www.theguardian.com/global-development/video/2012/aug/16/somali-refugee-sweden-video

Kordic, A. (2015, December 12). What is The Meaning Behind the New Banksy Piece in Calais? Retrieved September 26, 2018, from Widewalls website: https://www.widewalls.ch/banksy-steve-jobs-calais

Kristeva, J. (1982). *Powers of Horror: An Essay on Abjection* (Reprint edition; L. Roudiez, Trans.). New York, NY: Columbia University Press.

Lapowsky, I. (2015, December 11). Banksy's Steve Jobs Mural Misses the Point About Refugees. *Wired*. Retrieved from https://www.wired.com/2015/12/banksys-steve-jobs-mural-misses-the-point-about-refugees/

Matamoros, C. A. (2018, August 28). Venezuela exodus: "People are leaving in order to survive." Retrieved September 7, 2018, from euronews website: http://www.euronews.com/2018/08/28/venezuela-exodus-people-are-leaving-in-order-to-survive-

McRuer, R. (2002). Compulsory Able-Bodiedness and QueerlDisabled Existence. In S. Snyder, B. Brueggemann, & R. Garland-Thomson (Eds.), *Disability Studies: Enabling the Humanities*. New York: Modern Language Association.

Mulholland, R. (2016, January 22). Banksy mural of Steve Jobs defaced in Calais. *The Telegraph*. Retrieved from https://www.telegraph.co.uk/news/worldnews/europe/france/12115241/Banksy-mural-of-Steve-Jobs-defaced-in-Calais.html

Niles, C. A. (2018). Who gets in? The Price of Acceptance in Canada. *Journal of Critical Thought and Praxis*, *7*(1). https://doi.org/10.31274/jctp-180810-96

Philips, K. (2017, June 20). A Syrian artist's 'sweet revenge': Painting Trump and other world leaders as starving refugees. Retrieved September 27, 2018, from Washington Post website: https://www.washingtonpost.com/news/worldviews/wp/2017/06/20/a-syrian-artists-sweet-revenge-painting-trump-and-other-world-leaders-as-starving-refugees/

Qiblawi, T. (2017, June 13). Syrian artist depicts Trump and other leaders as refugees. Retrieved September 27, 2018, from CNN Style website: https://www.cnn.com/style/article/syrian-artist-depicts-trump-as-refugee/index.html

Rancière, J. (2009). *Aesthetics and Its Discontents*. Cambridge, UK; Malden, MA: Polity.

Rancière, J. (2011). *The Emancipated Spectator* (Reprint edition). London: Verso.

Roch, C. (2016, March 10). 7 free short films about refugees recommended by human rights educators. Retrieved September 27, 2018, from Amnesty International website: https://www.amnesty.org/en/latest/education/2016/03/seven-free-short-films-about-refugees-recommended-by-human-rights-educators/

Romanacce, T. (2017, June 19). Trump, Poutine, Assad, Sarkozy, Hollande... dans la peau de réfugiés syriens. Retrieved September 27, 2018, from FIGARO website: http://www.lefigaro.fr/culture/2017/06/19/03004-20170619ARTFIG00240-trump-poutine-assad-sarkozy-hollande-dans-la-peau-des-refugies-syriens.php

Ruechert, P. (2017, June 16). This Syrian Artist Is Depicting World Leaders as Refugees to Make a Very Important Point. Retrieved September 27, 2018, from Global Citizen website: https://www.globalcitizen.org/en/content/syrian-artist-world-leaders-refugees/

Sekerci, K., & Altiraifi, A. (2018, January 31). A US immigration history of white supremacy and ableism. Retrieved October 4, 2018, from https://www.aljazeera.com/indepth/opinion/immigration-history-white-supremacy-ableism-180122111928695.html

Sweet Revenge: Syrian Artist Turns World Leaders 'Vulnerable.' (n.d.). Retrieved October 2, 2018, from The Quint website: https://www.thequint.com/news-videos/2017/06/03/syrian-artist-vulnerability-series

Szary, A.-L. A. (2012). Walls and Border Art: The Politics of Art Display. *Journal of Borderlands Studies, 27*(2), 213–228. https://doi.org/10.1080/08865655.2012.687216

Tena, J. (2015, May 14). 10 Best Human Rights Videos. Retrieved September 27, 2018, from Amnesty International website: https://www.amnesty.org/en/latest/education/2015/05/10-best-human-rights-videos/

The Vulnerability Series [Artist website]. (n.d.). Retrieved September 27, 2018, from ABDALLA AL OMARI website: http://www.abdallaomari.com/thevulnerabilityseries/

Warren, R. (2013, June 12). They replaced black people with white to make you see this differently. Did it work? Retrieved September 28, 2018, from Upworthy website: https://www.upworthy.com/they-replaced-black-people-with-white-to-make-you-see-this-differently-did-it-work-2

Watts-Jones, D. (2002). Healing Internalized Racism: The Role of a Within-Group Sanctuary Among People of African Descent. *Family Process, 41*(4), 591–601. https://doi.org/10.1111/j.1545-5300.2002.00591.x

When you don't exist... (2012, September 10). Retrieved September 27, 2018, from Human Rights Channel website: https://www.coe.int/en/web/human-rights-channel/refugees-and-migration/videos/-/asset_publisher/j61mOEdcdaWp/content/when-you-don-t-exist-

Wilmer, S. E. (2018). *Performing Statelessness in Europe*. UK, Palgrave Macmillan

Young, I. M. (2011). *Justice and the Politics of Difference* (Revised ed. edition). Princeton, N.J: Princeton University Press.

CHAPTER 3

MANIFESTATIONS OF TRANSFER IN THE LATEST POST-YUGOSLAV PLAYWRITING AND THEATRE: MIGRATION, CULTURAL MOBILITY AND TRANSCULTURALITY

Gabriela Abrasowicz

Introduction

The impulse to cross geographical barriers and to go beyond boundaries, of whatever nature they might be, marks the history of humanity. So today, migrations, social remittances, and cultural transfer are not rare phenomena, but rather elements of daily life. They are the most effective factors in dissemination of ideas, signs, cultural artefacts, and codes, practices, skills, social capital, and identities. In the process of translocation from one cultural situation to another, all these components fall into a new context and take on a new meaning.

The increasingly more popular concept of "transfer" may be interpreted as a method of communication between communities and cultures. Its success depends on a few important factors: apart from causes and paths followed by particular influences, the "vessels" transposing the content and consequences of the whole process should be taken into account. Detailed analysis and appropriate record of data may help in creating a specific transactional map with its structural points of density. Significantly, transfer is a spontaneous process to a certain extent, and its "vessel may either be a human being or any human product" (Zajas, 2016: 22). As a result, these actions and reactions may produce completely new artistic qualities and social values. The research of cultural transfer ought to focus on proving the change of perspective, the occurrence of numerous links and phenomena of transgression, and the intermingling between the realms of culture (Mitterbauer as cited in Jabłkowska, 2013). Relocation and transformation are the characteristic features of the globalised twenty-first century society. These phenomena are the centre of artists' interest, but they have also a significant impact on how the broadly interpreted artistic expression is organised.

The process of moving from one country, region or place of residence to settle down in another and a series of long-term development processes of mutual cultural interferences are reflected in the latest dramatical and theatrical production in the semi-peripheral post-Yugoslav region. This manifested itself especially in the unique sphere of communication generated by the geopolitical situation in the former Yugoslavia and in new post-Yugoslav countries at the end of the twentieth century and beginning of the twenty-first: Bosnia and Herzegovina, Croatia, Kosovo, Macedonia, Montenegro, Serbia and Slovenia.

This mosaic of the post-Yugoslav region is the reflection of one of the key issues of the present: the tension between cultural homogenisation and cultural heterogenization and the globally binding idiom of multilingualism, multiethnicity, and multidenominationality, complex identity processes and dependencies. The phenomenon of transfer within the dramatical and theatrical production generated in that region may be discussed on different levels, which, to varying degrees, touch upon such processes as migration, cultural mobility and transcultural practices. In this view, both the literal – physical relocation – and metaphorical aspects are vital, which is tantamount to transposition of values, ideas or particular cultural goods from the original to the target context. The latter- thanks to this intervention- changes its from the nature (Borowski & Sugiera, 2016).

The term "post-Yugoslav" refers to a cultural concept, or to a particular economic-political realm (Matijević, 2016). This semi-peripheral position, entailing accumulation, liberation and flows, interlocks with the cultural policy and observation of cultural transfers.

These dynamics are essential for the status of post-Yugoslav cultural and literary discourse. It is a sound and necessary concept of cultural and literary theorisation and production. To talk about post-Yugoslav cultural space means to distance oneself implicitly from the isolationism and autarchy of the national(istic) cultures, and "see them as an open dynamic constellation" (Postnikov as cited in Matijević, 2016: 106). A sharp division between the centre and peripheries based on a binary opposition ceases to fit the currently changing cultural context.

It should be noted that in the meta-space of now non-existing Yugoslavia, art practices persist and communicate in the same space in which they were active before the demise of the state, and in which they had operated before its establishment (Popović & Belc, 2014). This region is like an "organism that is very complex and naturally decentralised, and yet closely interrelated in its segments by various events, working networks, and human ties, as well as the common aspiration to become part of an even wider (European, global) artistic context" (Denegri as cited in Popović & Belc, 2014: 19). The

Post-Yugoslav artistic domain is by no means a nostalgic attempt at the restoration of an old social project, but it comprises initiatives seeking to form a new network of cooperation and transfer.

There is no doubt that, at the turn of millennia, post-Yugoslav drama lends itself to stage production as its most valuable and recognisable intellectual export commodity in the micro- and macroscale. It is an attractive artistic medium pregnant with meaning successfully implemented by artists, who have lost their ideological, national, political, moral, and even metaphysical grounds of existence and experienced rarefied identity. The post-Yugoslav drama and theatre, transformed in the rhythm imposed by modernity, has undergone a radical qualitative revival, in the process becoming a more adequate medium of socially committed artistic expression. Artistic work causes reactions and calls for assuming responsibility, while feedback affects its form. Search for inspiration and new ways of expression were accompanied by a gradual move away from the nationalistic and xenophobic discourse imposed by the regime and the renouncement of conventional patterns of artistic expression.

The intraregional and international transfer seen in this artistic creation constitutes a bridge linking thematization of migration in playwriting and theatrical productions, the phenomenon of cultural mobility implemented by artists, and the expansion of a transcultural network. These overlapping domains will be discussed in this review of the latest artistic works exhibiting various transpositions and reflecting on the issue of identity.

Thematization of migration

Post-Yugoslav playwrights have examined migration as a phenomenon in a number of ways. Examples can be classified by type (e.g., by the reasons for migration, duration of relocation, and geographic distribution of the resettlement, etc.). Fates of migrants (who can be defined as immigrants and sojourners when the change in their location is voluntary) and refugees (whose movement is involuntarily - Berry, Poortinga, & Segall, 1992) are depicted in plays and shows produced in theses territories. The protagonists are placed at various stages of migration: pre-migration, involving the decision and preparation to move, physical relocation, and postmigration, or the absorption of the immigrant within the social and cultural framework of the new society. They are confronted with new social and cultural realities and adopt new roles out of necessity. The social stress of clashes in motives and values and the dynamics of the migrant's transformation undoubtedly attract the attention of playwrights and stage directors.

Contemporary playwriting in the region features a number of theatre projects about migration, which are a part of the artivistic trend emerging in these areas since the 1990s. Artivism operates at the intersection of the "expanded fields" of art and activism to create scenarios that advance social criticism. Artivists use their artistic talents to fight and struggle against injustice and oppression using any means necessary (Goris & Hollander, 2017). Material of this artistic message can be categorised. This field is dominated by texts on the socio-political dimensions of (sometimes illegal) migration, which is a consequence of war, political persecutions, ethnic conflicts, and related phenomena, e.g. ethnic cleansing, as well as disappearances of civilians.

Artists, who witnessed atrocities in the Balkans and elsewhere, expressed the urge to transform pictures of war; they did not necessarily focus on the obvious crimes against life and health of active participants in the events, but often they were inspired by the everyday experience of displaced civilians forced to flee.

This specific trend of artistic expression is a form of reaction to the events related to the exodus of people during the wars in Bosnia and Herzegovina and Kosovo, but also to other migration movements and the subsequent anti-refugee panic caused by a wave of immigrants from other geocultural zones (Syria or the Ukraine). Texts and theatre shows are frequently a kind of re-enactment of true events such as: oppression and discrimination, a threat to health and life, escape plans, being sent to refugee camps and attempts of inclusion in a new place. The term migration is also closely linked to the construction of the "**Other,**" in our everyday realities, in the media, and on stage. The uprooted person, the migrant figure, whether political, economic or spiritual, often triggers tensions between the familiar and the unknown, native and foreign, us and them.

The initiatives of documentary humanitarian interactive theatre are also put forward. These are mostly methods of developing a language that provides a critical awareness about trauma. Women who create the "HerStories" genre are a vast majority of the authors. They confirm the research of the Israeli sociologist Nira Yuval-Davies, who notes that exile is an experience strictly related to gender because most of the people who are forced to escape their countries are women and children (Yuval-Davis, 2003).

An important text about migration, where the painful experience is presented from a woman's perspective, is *All on board* (2004) by Bosnian author Jasna Šamić (1949, Sarajevo). The description of the fate of refugees and asylum-seekers combines with a critical commentary of cultural and social asymmetries of the contemporary world. The play is set on an old ship anchoring in a harbour in Denmark; its passengers are citizens of Bosnia and Herzegovina who were forced to leave their country. Their culture is rejected as it contradicts local codes. Their living space is restricted and controlled, while the experienced marginalization excludes the refugees from the sphere of meanings, which is tantamount to social non-existence (Dzido, 2006).

The protagonist of *The Acacia-Tree* (*Bagremovo drvo*, 2012) play grapples with social invisibility. The drama was written by Croatian author Lydia Scheuermann Hodak (1942, Osijek), who in 1992 wrote also a touching monodrama *Maria's Pictures* about a wartime rape (*Slike Marijine*). The unnamed Girl's confession evokes the loss of the father, farewell from the mother, and life in detention and refugee camps. The protagonist continuously changes places, but none offers stability. Ultimately, after suffering a string of humiliations at the hands of her employers, the Girl resigns herself to temporary degradation and returns to the camp, where she will build up her strength to reconstruct her identity.

The authors emphasize also the fact that female migrants fall victim to deceit and sexual exploitation. Croatian playwright Diana Meheik (1987, Zagreb), who witnessed a media frenzy following the death of a Ukrainian prostitute Olena Popik, decided to break the conspiracy of silence and highlight the issue of human trafficking and procuration. In her play *The Rose of Jericho* (*Jerihonska ruža*, 2007) a woman grapples with the world as an eternal stranger, homeless both in metaphorical and literary sense. She strays like a desert plant, lonely and living in cycles. Because of her way of life, she cannot find a firm ground and put down roots. Already at the beginning of her journey, she falls victim of criminal gangs and, ultimately, excessively exploited and ailing, she is placed in a hospital in Mostar (quite significantly, human trafficking in Bosnia and Herzegovina was an exceptionally profitable business tolerated by UN peacekeeping forces).

There are also works presenting a broader picture of the problems which affects practically everybody, regardless of gender and age. Uprooting a person from the familiar surroundings, which formed his or her relations, skills, habits, and predilections leads to difficulties experienced in transferring them to a new environment, which has to be adapted to, entailing a risk of marginalization, degradation and disintegration. This is very suggestively presented by Croatian Tena Štivičić (1977, Zagreb) in her play *Fragile!* (2007). The drama combines fates of Balkan immigrants, fleeing the war and its consequences, with stories of victims of human trafficking throughout the western world. The new inhabitants of London function in a separate, parallel world. Even though they communicate in English and strive to begin a new chapter in life, they are unable to forget the dramatic past haunting them. It turns out that the only place where they may settle (both in the physical and symbolic senses) is the area impossible to tame, the land of exclusion. The story of hardships of integrating people who lost virtually everything in the war, including the prospects for a better life, is told in Štivičić's latest play *Invisible* (Nevidljivi, 2016).

An interesting study of the theme is *Belgrade Trilogy* (*Beogradska trilogija*, 1997) written by Biljana Srbljanović (1970, Stockholm). The Serbian playwright returned to the theme in her later dramas: *Supermarket* (2001) and *America, Part Two* (*Amerika, drugi deo*, 2003). Her dramatic texts depict a person entering into a sphere of increasing alienation. The characters become little more than a cog in the machine or an individual disturbing the social and aesthetic orders, which is tantamount to restricting social relations to extreme ritualization, limited forms of interaction, and increased isolation.

Texts "about children but not for children" where a motif of a journey appears are yet another subgroup. They youngest witnesses of war atrocities are forced to wander the world aimlessly; they feel lonely and lost in a new place; this issue is superbly presented by Bosnian writer Tanja Šljivar (1988, Banja Luka) in her play *Scratching or How My Grandmother Killed Herself* (*Grebanje ili Kako se ubila moja baka*, 2012). Serbian playwright Milan Marković (1978, Belgrade) in his text *Maya and me and Maya* (*Maja i ja i Maja*, 2012) and an artist from Kosovo, Jeton Neziraj (1977, Kaçanik), also explore the motif of emigration, repatriation and searching for a place where one belongs) in plays such as *Yue Madeleine Yue* (2014) and *The Windmills* (*Die Windmühlen*, 2017). Scenes of children's brutalised games and everyday problems emphasize the fact that they experience increased alienation.

Socio-economic immigration – connected with striving for improvement of the living and social standards is also a theme frequently taken up in plays and performances. Protagonists of these plays realise that climbing a social ladder abroad will require sacrifice. Often their double affiliation and double identity result in absence of the sense of belonging and distinct identity, a suspension "in-between", and a feeling of uncertainty and incompleteness. They feel claustrophobic in their familiar surroundings. Economic migrants are often forced to reject their roots. An important issue in these works is a gastarbeiter returning home and confronting the abandoned – but no longer their own – reality, with expectations of close relatives. It is often accompanied by a sense of frustration and disappointment. This motif appears, e.g. in the works of Serbian writers Uglješa Šajtinac (1971, Zrenjanin) – *Huddersfield* (2004) and Dušan Spasojević (1980, Valjevo) – *Withering* (*Odumiranje*, 2006).

The authors present some scenes from the migrants' life, which create a taboo-breaking mosaic image. It is possible thanks to using relations and interviews as the primary basis, and involving migrants and their close relatives or witnesses in the creation process. The authors emphasize that migrating people come from diverse cultural backgrounds, with cultural identities already formed. Cultural changes in identity can be stressful and result in problems with self-esteem and mental health. Contact between the immigrant, or minority community with the dominant or host community may lead to assimilation, rejection, integration or deculturation. Migration prompts the characters to grapple with a variety of contradictions of hospitality and hostility, of solidarity and security, of activism and passivity, of movement and stasis.

Playwrights and theatre directors who use these texts look at images of migrants carefully and tenderly without any resort to fearful enclosure or worn out clichés. They try to show not only that the phenomenon of migration could be perceived outside of the frame defined by television journalists or populist politicians, but also, that this perception could produce intriguing and multifarious effects.

Cultural mobility

It is impossible to discuss theatre in isolation from the mobile nature of culture; after all it is subject to mechanisms related to relocation and change of contexts. Nowadays a common denominator for many stage performances (and similarly for dramatic texts) is not a language, memory, or history. Creating a cultural reality through dramatic literature and theatre means an intense use of a specific cultural tradition in unity with needs and expectations formulated by new users, according to the principle of filling gaps. Transplanted into a new ground, they gain new functions and meanings.

Social and economic changes opened more efficient channels of communication and mobility, which resulted in expanding the perspectives for the authors and shifted the paradigm of artistic creation. Another theme which appears in the artistic creations of the authors of the middle and younger generation is journeying in order to acquire knowledge and new experiences, collect sensations, and carry out existential searches. These are works in which metaphors of journey and road are used to describe problems of twenty-first century societies, but they often have an autobiographical dimension as well. These are connected not only to consumption and hedonistic lifestyle but also to the private need to explore new places. The globalisation trend and the specific world view and context of mobility become clear through artistic residences, scholarships, and cooperation within international projects.

It is worth emphasizing that nomadism of artists is increasing; artists are also beneficiaries (or possibly victims? Similarly, as forced migrants?) of mobile globalisation. The playwrights from the countries of former Yugoslavia no longer write their plays in isolation; increasingly, they cross the borders of their countries, establishing contacts with their foreign fellow artists. This kind of mobility gives an opportunity to creators and cultural professionals to exchange knowledge, skills and experiences through direct contact, but also to get familiar with cultural systems of other environments. Another very important thing when it comes to mobility is that in this way artists are geared towards joint creation of contents (Tadić, 2017) within bigger projects. This phenomenon was heralded by first visits of playwrights from Serbia and Montenegro in the Royal Court Theatre in London (e.g., Maja Pelević, Milena Marković, Igor Bojović).

Since then an increasing trans-territorial circulation may be observed; this generates new perception of reality and new artistic expression, which is substantiated by the works written by Milena Bogavac (Serbia, *Ballerina/Gamma Cas – Balerina/Gamma Cas*, 2007); Maja Pelević and Olga Dimitrijević (Serbia, *Freedom: The Most Expensive Capitalist Word –* **Sloboda** *je* **najskuplja** *kapitalistička reč*, 2017); Goran Ferčec (Croatia, *Letter to Heiner M. – Pismo Heineru M.*, 2007), Tanja Šljivar (Bosnia and Herzegovina, *Ali grad me je štitio – But the city has protected me*, 2016), Jeton Neziraj (Kosovo, *The Demolition of the Eiffel Tower – Shembja e kullës së Ajfelit*, 2013). Some perspectives induce the reflection on the similarity of the fate of migrants and artists, and the double isolation of migrating artists.

Their work was then well received locally, but their artistic stance gradually changed, evolving into the attitude of openness, the urge to emerge from the shadow of isolation and accept external influence. Currently, the authors have a chance to become recognised in a wider context thanks to the activity of the centres coordinating and supporting their activity and cooperation. The work of playwrights is also promoted thanks to the tradition of competitions and festivals of international significance. In addition, intensive development of global ties and innovative technology of virtual distance communication promotes selected works on the international scale faster than ever.

Even though they identify themselves with their homeland, certain authors are more active abroad. They yield to being incorporated into a circulation of a different culture (often Western), but they do not abandon their cultural background connected with the local territory known to them. The best-known playwrights of this trend are Tena Štivičić, Ivana Sajko and Ivor Martinić (Croatia), Milan Marković and Ana Lasić (Serbia), Žanina Mirčevska (Macedonia), Tanja Šljivar (Bosnia and Herzegovina). Some of them transform their impressions from the journeys and shorter or longer stays in the so-far unknown destinations into an artistic raw material. Themes in their works prompt reflection on the identity issues and transition from the "world of roots" to the "world of choice". In the modern world, the identity is aptly defined as dispersed, uprooted or hybrid, based on the combination of elements originally considered inconsistent. Marked with alienation and lack of stability, it belongs to the reality that escapes the inherited language of description. An idiosyncratic type of freedom and distance is presented by a theatre director, Oliver Frljić (1976, Travnik).

The work by "a travelling scandalmonger" is associated with the process of relocation, continual self-creation, deconstruction, and choice. Born in Bosnia (from the Croatian father and Serbian mother), Frljić himself was a refugee, was at the university in Croatia and directed in theatres in Croatia; he works regularly in Serbia and Slovenia as well as in Western Europe. He is a special case of an artist-researcher, who made conflict his main theme and tool and, who —in search of freedom to construct the identity and express thoughts—transgresses the boundaries and destroys fossilised structures. His latest projects, where the issue of forced relocation is pivotal, deserve attention. In *Gorki – Alternative for Germany?* (2018), actors from the Gorki Theatre (with Eastern European names) challenge each other and the audience by hurling political accusations, emotional complaints about current politics and institutions, and petty personal attacks into the open space. In *Second Exile* (2017), Frljić looks back on a time period of more than 20 years, since he first came to German soil as an asylum seeker back in 1995. Together with actors from Germany and former Yugoslavia, he positions individual destinies in relation to the global refugee crisis.

Playwrights and theatre producers explore new themes, new theatrical styles or new dramatic voices, they search for artistic fulfilment, new audiences. Without that there would have been no innovation in the dramatic art and theatre. Such activity implies change, translation, re-situation or re-location, adaptation, transferral, as well as embracement of the new. It fits into the framework of cultural mobility, a process that literary historian Stephen Greenblatt associates with the increasing transnational and transcultural flow of texts, habits, customs (Greenblatt, 2010). This notion, understood both in its literal and metaphorical senses, is exceptionally useful while searching for local regularities in the chaos of contemporary phenomena, readily globalised in terms of binary opposition, but it also introduces indispensable movement in excessively systematised traditional spheres (Borowski & Sugiera, 2016). It is surely desirable in case of observation of the contemporary development of playwriting and theatrical production in the post-Yugoslav region.

At the end of the twentieth century, mobility was in the function of political aspirations at the level of internal processes, "cultural diplomacy", and the presentation of predetermined desirable artistic production. The aim was to shape Western European artistic and public opinion of the social processes in the Balkan countries (Vujadinović, 2008). The mobility is mostly conditioned by a residence program for artists and cultural professionals. The phenomenon of the centralisation of information and availability of contacts can easily be noticed in big cities, especially the capitals, where cultural life is more intensive with activities of the embassies, foreign cultural centres, ministries, and company agencies (Vujadinović, 2008).

In recent years, possibilities of the regional mobility of artists and cultural professionals have increased and the most serious impediments dominant in the previous period have been overcome. Thanks to this, cultural cooperation in the region provides a unique opportunity for stimulation of creative potentials and provides a favourable environment for building "cultural bridges." Building relationships and establishing connections between very different artists, authors, and thinkers can improve communication between societies of the former Yugoslavia, but also to talk creatively about the topics that are difficult for our society. During this process, institutions like Heartefact Fund (Hartefakt Fond, Belgrade), *Dramaturgical Collective* (Dramaturški kolektiv, Zagreb) or Multimedia Centre (Qendra Multimedia, Pristina) have developed several platforms which aim to launch and affirm young authors from the region and throughout Europe.

Mobility requires institutional support, implementation of regulations of external organisations, an increase of awareness and knowledge about the conditions and procedures, which has enabled eliminating numerous obstacles restricting concluding contracts on intraregional scale and beyond.

Entering international teams and working on international artistic projects is possible thanks to travelling, the swinging movement between the homeland and the country of destination. On the other hand, thanks to electronic media, there is a peculiar disassembly of geography as a spatial, territorial base of culture, and simultaneously, the exceptionally passable and effective cross-border communication channels are being developed. In some areas of the reality, there is a mechanism that separates culture from geography; it creates the world filled with drifting cultures without specific spaces and people taken away from places. The escalation of these practices induces revision of the concept of playwriting and national theatre, as well as reflecting on the nature of the cross-border reality and the cross-border, hybrid identity in the drama and theatre world.

Mobility leading to interaction between the previously identified cultures may be indeed described as transfer. Many post-Yugoslav playwrights and directors are open to a "risky experience," to wandering on the boundaries of their own culture and its crossroads with other cultures. Planned, voluntary migrations, encounters, and interactions necessitating a confrontation with the Otherness, in the face of which one has to redefine oneself, are beneficial. However, what is essential is not so much a transfer from one cultural order to another, but a change in perception and thinking. The transfer in question is primarily a change of perspective in viewing the culture. Ethnic and national orders are only one of the spheres where actual cultural existence of a human being is taking place.

Transculturality

Transfers determine also existence of the transcultural migration theatre. We can talk about the tendency to create new hybrid qualities and transcultural network in case of dramatic and theatrical production in the region. Cultures were neither in the past, nor they are in the present, static constitutions. They have changed somehow either because of internal or external dynamics. The phenomena perceptible in the contemporary sphere of drama and theatre, whose basic premise – after all – is encounter and interaction, testify to the circulation and combination of elements from various cultures.

The shift to cooperation and exchange in the post-Yugoslav region was not automatic and obvious after a period of visible division and emphasizing the cultural identities of the newly-formed countries. However, one can notice clearer and clearer signs which prove a trend towards artistic migration and transposition of ideas. Theatrical projects which have developed as a result of the transposition of artistic, socio-political and philosophical ideas and the physical movement of artists are important intersection junctions in the regional transcultural network powered by institutions.

In its cultural aspect, the analysis of the condition of contemporary post-Yugoslav playwriting and theatre at the turn of millennia should refer to the network of notions employing the trans-element such as transfer, transaction, trans-border, transformation, and translation. Transdisciplinary approach allows to create a complex innovative description as well as to supplement one's knowledge about migration with new semantic contexts.

The concept of transculturality and dynamic model of open links (based on the concept of the German postmodernist theorist Wolfgang Welsch) is most adequate while contemplating the formation of new ethical paradigms that influence the aspects of identity and culture in the post-Yugoslav region. Welsch criticised multiculturalism or even interculturalism because it uses "a conception of cultures as islands or spheres" (Deja, 2015: 92), creating a separatist character of cultures. Transcultural perspective is linked to an earlier concept of transculturation formulated by a Cuban anthropologist Fernando Ortiz. Thanks to the German philosopher, this notion has been transferred to and revived in Europe. The image of clash and mutual penetration of cultures and emergence of a new quality is tightly connected with the model of the network. It is a key element in the reflection on multi-dimensional, eclectic, hybrid nature of the artistic practices in the semi-peripheral post-Yugoslav region (Deja, 2015). This position and location in the zone between core integration and the logic of quasi-monopoly and destabilisation as well as exploitation of peripheries (Hughson & Stevanović, 2015) gives the opportunity to combine the potentials and generate projects based on regional cooperation.

Currently, among playwrights and theatre producers from the countries of former Yugoslavia, there is a strong tendency to initiate regional and international artistic cooperation. We can observe a prelude to artistic reorientation, a change from extremely heterogeneous art to the activities facilitating transposition and connectivity. In this way a foundation of new theatre is formed: local but still open to the flows of ideas. The dynamics of civilisation changes and the contemporary mechanism of intermingling cultures resulted in creating a specific transcultural post-Yugoslav network. It is not an isolated case, but a certain variant of universal changes. It shall be stressed however, that it is surprising taking into account the language, ethnic, mentality, cultural and religious diversities and the already mentioned conflicts arising from these differences.

A number of projects— more or less experimental in their nature— have been implemented in the region; they are not grounded solely in the fact of translation or mutual inspiration, but they are artistic endeavours proving that a promising model of cooperation has been worked out. The adopted strategy enables transmission of ideas, transposition of cultural patterns, and articulation of source content in an absolutely novel way. A Serbian playwright and performer, Milena Bogavac calls these undertakings "bypassing" (originally, she uses this phrase to describe a cardiac surgical operation, in the title of one of her works Bypass Serbia). The number of such undertakings, perceived as turning points in the development of transcultural post-Yugoslav theatre, is constantly growing. Therefore, co-creation related to the transfer and arising out of productive communication among playwrights, dramatists, directors, actors, and producers from Serbia, Croatia, Bosnia and Hercegovina, Montenegro, Macedonia and Kosovo ceases to surprise. Examples of playwriting-theatrical networking keep multiplying. Artistic proposals are better thought through, refined, sometimes bilingual. Intensification of these activities seems to be inevitable and certainly is optimistic and encouraging.

The material in this area has been elaborated as a part of the research project "(Trans)Position of Ideas in Croatian and Serbian Playwriting and Theatre (1990-2020). A Transcultural Perspective" (No. 2017/24/C/HS2/00436) implemented at the University of Silesia and financed by the National Science Centre in Poland. In response to the need of organising the material, including the transcultural perspective and networking aspects, an establishment of a new website with database is planned. It will be an element supporting quantitative and qualitative analysis of the transcultural network comprising post-Yugoslav drama and theatre after the year 1990 and an optimal way of presenting dependencies, transfers and transpositions in this research area. A combination of traditional methods with modern digital technology will result in a more comprehensive and multifaceted view of the phenomenon. The project's webpage (http://www.transpozycjeidei.us. edu.pl/) may also become a platform for communication between researchers, opening new perspectives and a new path for the humanities.

Conclusion

Contemporary drama and theatre are acquiring new significance, requiring reconsideration and reinterpretation as a document of social changes, a mirror of political views and philosophical beliefs and also as an intervention.

The latest post-Yugoslav playwriting and theatre are developing in accordance with the rhythm of current globalisation processes and changes in the structure of power. The phenomena such as population movements caused by civilizational, military or economic factors, struggle for human rights, including the rights of all minorities to exist and express their identities, multicultural (but also transcultural) nature of the world, its hybridisation and cross-linking have significantly affected their thematic and formal aspects, distribution system and prestige. The comprehensive concept of transfer is best suited to perceive and characterise them.

The issue of the transfer in the theatre in the post-Yugoslav region may be considered in several correlated categories: thematization of migration, cultural mobility, transculturality and networking as a tactic of creation. The theatre about migration, and created thanks to migration, is the common denominator of dramatic and theatrical production in the post-Yugoslav region. Stories about the physical transfer of people and the cultural transfer are the issues that mesh as creative subjects and tactics. Social and cultural exchange connected with migration is not the circulation of objects and ideas as they already are, but their relentless reinterpretation, rethinking and re-signification.

The most representative examples presented in this review are a form of reaction, but they also testify to the interesting changes on the cultural map of Europe, increasingly intensive involvement of authors and workers of the cultural sector in overcoming various barriers, which is seen in the sources of inspiration, transcultural reflection and the adopted attitude of openness. This artistic creation transpires to be an especially forceful and effective factor supporting a constructive dialogue, understanding, and common creative effort.

In addition, it is necessary to bear in mind the fact that it is migrants and nomads, not autochthons who enrich the culture. Arts and culture certainly need stability, but above all they need development whereby the issues of difference and sameness, locality and globality, in-rootedness and out-rootedness determine the cultural practice.

The preliminary research, which so far can be drawn on transfers, exchange, integration and transformation components of various cultural origins in post-Yugoslav drama and theatre, encourages further research in this field.

References

Berry, J., Poortinga, Y., & Segall, M. (Eds.). (1992). Cross cultural psychology: research and applications. Cambridge: Cambridge University Press.

Bhugra, D. (2001). Acculturation, cultural identity and mental health. In R. Cochrane (Ed.), Psychiatry in multicultural Britain (pp. 112-136). London: Gaskell.

Borowski, M., & Sugiera, M. (2016). Transfer kulturowy czy kulturowa mobilność: rekonesans teoretyczny. In M. Leyko & A. Pełka (Eds.), Teatr – Literatura – Media. O polsko-niemieckich oddziaływaniach w sferze kultury po 1989 roku (pp. 43-43). Łódź: Primum Verbum.

Deja, K. (2015). Transkulturowość: od koncepcji Wolfganga Welscha do transkulturowej historii literatury. WIELOGŁOS. Pismo Wydziału Polonistyki UJ, 4 (26), 87-107. doi: 10.4467/2084395XWI.15.034.5151

Dzido, D. (2006). Kulturowe kody płci. In J. M. Kurczewski, B. Łaciak, A. Herman, D. Dzido & A. Suflida (Eds.), Praktyki cielesne (pp. 198-212). Warszawa: Trio.

Goris, Y., & Hollander, S. (Eds.). (2017). Activism, Artivism and Beyond. Inspiring initiatives of civic power. Retrieved from https://www.dedikkeblauwe.nl/files/attachment/715.

Greenblatt, S. (Ed.). (2010). Cultural Mobility: A Manifesto. New York: Cambridge University Press.

Hughson, M., & Stevanović, Z. (2015). Kriminal i društvo Srbije: izazovi društvene dezintegracije, društvene regulacije i očuvanja životne sredine. Beograd: Institut za kriminološka i sociološka istraživanja.

Jabłkowska, J. (2016). Transfer kulturowy czy po prostu kontakty? In M. Leyko & A. Pełka (Eds.), Teatr – Literatura – Media. O polsko-niemieckich oddziaływaniach w sferze kultury po 1989 roku (pp. 26-42). Łódź: Primum Verbum.

Matijević, T. (2016). National, post-national, transnational. Is post-Yugoslav literature an arguable or promising field of study? In N. Frieß, G. Lenz & E. Martin (Eds.), Grenzräume–Grenzbewegungen: Ergebnisse der Arbeitstreffen des Jungen Forums Slavistische Literaturwissenschaft Basel 2013, Frankfurt (Oder) und Slubice 2014 (pp. 101-112). Leipzig: Universitätsverlag.

Pick, D. (2013). Czym jest transfer kultury? Transfer kultury a metoda porównawcza. Możliwości zastosowania transferts culturels na gruncie polski. In M. Zielińska & M. Zybura (Eds.), Monolog, dialog, transfer. Relacje kultury polskiej i niemieckiej w XIX i XX wieku (pp. 255-268). Wrocław: Instytut Willy`ego Brandta.

Popović, M., & Belc, P. (2014). Jugonostalgija: Jugoslavija kao metaprostor u suvremenim umjetničkim praksama. Život umjetnosti: časopis za suvremena likovna zbivanja, 94 (1), 18-35. Retrieved from https://hrcak.srce.hr/185597

Romanowska, J. (2013). Transkulturowość czy trankulturacja? O perypetiach pewnego bardzo modnego terminu. Zeszyty Naukowe Towarzystwa Doktorantów UJ. Nauki Humanistyczne, 6 (1), 143-153. Retrieved from https://ruj.uj.edu.pl

Tadić, D. (2017). Creative Europe Programme as an Instrument of European Cooperation, Internationalisation and Strengthening the Capacity of Cultural Organisations and Institutions in Serbia. In M. Dragićević Šešić (Ed.) Cultural Diplomacy: Arts, Festivals and Geopolitics (pp. 265-274). Belgrade: Desk.

Vujadinović, B. (2008). Mobility of Artists and Cultural Professionals in South Eastern

Europe. Retrieved from http://nck.pl/badania/raporty/mobility-of-artists-and-cultural-professionals-in-south-eastern-europe

Yuval-Davis, N. (2003). Nacionalistički projekti i rodni odnosi. Treća, Časopis Centra za ženske studije, 5 (1-2), 208-233. Retrieved from https://hrcak.srce.hr/file/52677

Zajas, P. (2016). Niemilknące muzy. Wydawcy, pisarze, tłumacze i pośrednicy kulturowi na frontach Wielkiej Wojny 1914-1918. Poznań: Wydawnictwo Naukowe Uniwersytetu im. Adama Mickiewicza.

CHAPTER 4

MIGRANTS, IDENTITY, AND BODY MODIFICATION IN BIBLICAL AND ANCIENT NEAR EASTERN MEDIA

Eric Trinka

Introduction

The biblical account of Joseph's experience is one of human trafficking and forced migration. To date, much attention has been given to Joseph's apparent upward economic and occupational success, as well as his social mobility through processes of willful assimilation once in the House of Pharaoh. This limits of this well-rehearsed reading of the text are shown here as I focus on a particular moment of Joseph's experience in Egypt that has to date received sparse attention: his shaving activity before his presentation to Pharaoh as a dream interpreter. The account of Joseph's life is read here as an exilic (*golah*) response to the reality of Judahite relocation to Babylon and Egypt. I show that the seemingly unimportant mention of Joseph shaving prior to his meeting with Pharaoh is not merely a presentation of his aesthetic self-preparation, but a representation of purposeful body modification and a statement about Joseph's behavior as a Hebrew residing in a foreign land. The story is, as such, an instructive narrative for a migrant audience working out their own crises of identity in foreign contexts.

A deeper analytical exercise can be undertaken when one considers that there is more than one ancient version of the Joseph story. Different migrant communities possessed the story and adapted it to their specific contexts. To illuminate these differences, I set the Hebrew version, which was primarily conceived by and for Babylonian and Judean audiences, in conversation with the Greek version, a later translation, produced in Egypt by and for diasporic Judeans living there. Through this juxtaposition, one can read the Hebrew version as leveling a critique against Joseph's assimilative behaviors. On the other hand, the Greek version of the same text constitutes a response to the earlier Hebrew *Vorlage* and tempers those critiques by making translational choices that defer the responsibility of Joseph's Egyptianizing body modifications away from him and place the onus on his captors. The stylized motifs of bodily presentation in both versions play on the popular media depictions of Egyptian cultural norms and mobile peoples of the time.

The analysis offered in this chapter is literary in nature. It does not present an argument for or against the historical veracity of the events described, nor does it require the historical existence of an actual Joseph. Both texts play on commonly known tropes found in visual and written media across the ancient Near East. The preservation of Joseph's story indicates a rich cultural memory for its authors and the communities that passed it on over millennia along with various accompanying interpretations. This exposition asks what literary or historiographical depictions of voluntary and forced migrants reveal, intentionally or unintentionally, about the authors responsible for their production and the audience(s) intended as their recipients.

Applying research on migrant assimilation and acculturation to the reading of Genesis 41 illuminates its role as an internal social critique of assimilative behavior and a prescriptive text for Judean identity preservation in the midst of Babylonian contexts. Furthermore, research on the myriad ways modern migrant communities work out religious differences, especially concerning issues of acculturation and integration, provides helpful means for engaging these ancient texts. We are able to see that the very issues migrant communities deal with are indeed ancient but not outdated. Not only does reading through the lens of modern migration studies makes us better readers of these ancient texts, it also makes us more adept researchers of the intersection of migrants and media in our own contexts.

The Joseph Story in/and Two Bibles

The Joseph story is well-known and does not require extensive introduction. A summary of the its main contours will suffice. The Hebrew narrative begins with an account of Joseph's distinction from his brothers through his faculties as a dream interpreter. His own dream that he will surpass his brothers in greatness is augmented by his father's preference for him among all of his sons. His father, Jacob—who is also the namesake of the people Israel—makes his privileging of Joseph officially known when he gifts Joseph a robe "with sleeves" (translated in the Greek as a robe "of many colors"). The significance of such a garment is that it is the clothing of one with authority, and thus upsets the patrimonial systems of fraternal order in ancient Near Eastern societies.

One day, young Joseph is sent by his father to attend his shepherding brothers in the fields. Seizing the opportunity to eliminate the threat that this young dreamer poses to their inheritance, the brothers conspire to kill Joseph. They almost accomplish this goal, but Judah, the oldest brother intervenes and suggests that they fake Joseph's death and sell him instead to a passing caravan of Ishmaelites/Midianites. By this maneuver, Joseph ends up in Egypt, sold into the home of Potiphar, an Egyptian noble with direct associations to the Pharaoh. Joseph meets with great success during his time in Potiphar's house, but his youth and stature draw the unwanted attention of Potiphar's wife, who desires Joseph for herself. He escapes her advances only to be falsely charged with adultery and ends up imprisoned in the Pharaoh's house.

The story continues with Joseph's time in prison, where his dream-interpreting skills earn him a reputation. One of his fellow prisoners who benefited from Joseph's gifts of dream interpretation recalls Joseph's abilities at an important juncture when the Pharaoh himself is in need of explanations for his own troubling dreams. The Pharaoh solicits Joseph's talents and summons him in Genesis 41 to offer assistance in interpreting a series of recurring dreams. Since this call comes to Joseph while he is in prison, he must ready himself to appear before Pharaoh. The Hebrew text describes the series of events that constitute Joseph's self-preparation:

וַיִּשְׁלַח פַּרְעֹה וַיִּקְרָא אֶת־יוֹסֵף וַיְרִיצֻהוּ מִן־הַבּוֹר וַיְגַלַּח וַיְחַלֵּף שִׂמְלֹתָיו וַיָּבֹא אֶל־פַּרְעֹה׃

"Then Pharaoh sent for Joseph, and he was hurriedly brought out of the dungeon. When he had shaved himself and changed his clothes, he came in before Pharaoh."
(Genesis 41:14)

The Greek version of the account is slightly, but meaningfully, different:

Ἀποστείλας δὲ Φαραω ἐκάλεσεν τὸν Ιωσηφ, καὶ ἐξήγαγον αὐτὸν ἐκ τοῦ ὀχυρώματος καὶ ἐξύρησαν αὐτὸν καὶ ἤλλαξαν τὴν στολὴν αὐτοῦ, καὶ ἦλθεν πρὸς Φαραω.
"Then Pharao sent for and called Ioseph, and they brought him out of the stronghold and shaved him and changed his apparel, and he came to Pharao."

According to the Greek version of the story, Joseph is shaved, and his clothing changed by those bringing him before Pharaoh. This is contrary to the Hebrew text, wherein he shaves himself and changes his own clothing. The difference in agentic focus between these accounts should not be overlooked. The use of third person plural verbs in the Greek text subtly removes responsibility of shaving and changing from Joseph and places it on the attendants. Thus, in the Greek, his captors are the ones who "Egyptianize" him rather than him doing it to himself.

The Joseph Story: Text(s) and Context(s)

The origin of the Joseph story and its respective dates of composition are unknown. It is possible that the core of the narrative, an account of a Hebrew sold into slavery in Egypt, is quite ancient and relays the socio-political situation that attended the lives of tribal populations living in the Levant in the Middle through Late Bronze and Early Iron Ages. These periods experienced a remarkable level of inter-regional mobility that included forced and voluntary population movements made possible by powerful imperial states that coexisted through commerce and complex gift economies which included royal inter-marriage and the exchange of courtiers. At the margins of each of these imperial entities were populations of social outcasts, tribal groups, and vassal kingdoms that supported and were supported by unequal but mutually-beneficial associations with larger actors (Van De Mieroop, 2004). It is in such a context that the Joseph story is narratively situated, even though the periods of redaction for the versions explored here are well after Bronze and Iron age realities supposed in the tale.

Several historical realities have come to bear between the earliest instantiations of the Joseph story and the forms we read today. Egypt's dominance over the Levant waned significantly by the beginning of the Iron Age, and subsequent Assyrian and Babylonian military campaigns upended the smaller ethnically-defined polities that had arisen in the region during that same time. Among these, the northern kingdom of Israel—the original tradent of the Joseph story—was decimated by the Assyrians. Within a century, Assyria would fall and be replaced by Babylon who would exact their own imperial agenda on the Levant that included the conquest of the southern kingdom of Judah and its capital Jerusalem. By this moment in history—typically known singularly as the Babylonian Exile, though it took place over the course of three campaigns in 597, 587/6, and 582/1 BCE—the contents of the Joseph story were already part of the religious texts and traditions that Judah had inherited from Israel (Fleming, 2012).

Following the Babylonian-instigated forced migrations of the sixth century, geographically-dispersed communities that shared these common religious texts continued their existences in new locations. Diasporic communities arose in multiple places around the Mediterranean, but the three primary population centers were Babylon, where a portion of Judean elites were exiled; Egypt, where large contingents of escapees had resettled and organized as a semi-autonomous polity; and the land of Judah (known later under Persian rule as Yehud), where those unwilling or unable to leave remained along with persons who had relocated, both forcefully and voluntarily, to the Levant at various points during the Assyrian, Babylonian, and Persian periods. Yehud would also become home to a small contingent of Judahite returnees from Babylon during the Persian reign of Cyrus. The redaction of the Joseph story now contained in the Hebrew Bible took place sometime during the Babylonian or Persian periods among the Judean population in Babylon.

Having taken common narratives of a shared ancestral origins into various locations, the different groups continued to draw on and amend them in distinct ways that responded to their new contexts. Among other things, these narrative traditions were means of identity pronouncement and negotiation. Thus, in addition to the version of the Joseph story that exists in Hebrew Bible, we also have a Greek-language version of the story that is part of a translation of the Hebrew texts for Egyptian-Judean communities that no longer spoke or read Hebrew known as the *Septuagint*. The earliest instance of this Greek translation project came to be ca. 250 BCE, at least 250 years after the Babylonian redaction of Joseph story (Dines, 2004). The creators of this Greek bible translated their ancestral Hebrew texts with great care. Yet, the work of translation always requires interpretation and decisions about previous meaning in new contexts. Thus, throughout the *Septuagint*, we find evidence of translational choices that reflect the environments and commitments of their translators. These include purposeful changes that are responsive to the specific contexts of reception in the extra-Judean environments of Egypt during the Persian and Hellenistic Periods. Several such instances of textual modification are apparent within the Joseph story.

These literary depictions of a common ancestor capture processes of communal discernment regarding ethnicity, boundary-marking, assimilation and acculturation in real time. The various presentations of Joseph's identity negotiation presented in these biblical accounts is representative of the internal negotiations taking place among authorial communities. Though Joseph himself may have never existed, the worldviews he represents in the two versions of his story certainly played out in direct contest with one another in the ancient world. The remainder of this chapter explores how the differences between the two versions of the story can be understood in light of migration studies and acculturation research. In an effort to show that the narrative event of Joseph's shaving was no trivial matter for its audiences, I turn first to an exposition of the symbolic importance of hair in the ancient Near East, its association with foreigners in Egypt, and depictions of hair removal in ancient Near Eastern media. This is followed by a brief review of the data concerning migrant identity negotiation and hair removal practices in the acculturative matrix. Before concluding, I draw the comparative lens back to explore other elements of body modification presented in the Joseph story in order to elucidate the larger conversations about migrants and acculturation preserved across biblical texts.

Hair-Removal, Foreigners, and Migrants in/and Ancient Near Eastern Media

From very early in our existence, humans have responded to the presence of body hair in different ways. Cutting, dying, and styling hair on both the face and head has been common practice across the millennia (Kirchoff & Kitson, 2013). Archaeological remains from more than 30,000 years ago evidence the purposeful removal of hair (Fernandez, 2013). Hair maintenance, styling, and removal generally have attendant social meanings, and each is often associated with ethnic identity.

While ancients did not understand the concept of ethnicity according the anthropological categories of modern social scientists, the notions that one's identity was informed by their place of birth, kin relations, and physical appearance held purchase. States in the ancient world, as much as those in modern contexts, promoted the notion of identity as an essential concept. People groups maintained distinctive identity markers that included diet, language, physical appearance, material culture, and an array of norms that guided emic and etic relationships. Stereotypes of ethnicity were widespread in the ancient Near East and broadly depicted in various forms of media from imperial architecture to personalized artwork on burial goods. The person, as an ethnically identifiable member of a particular class who was associated with a particular geography, was made intelligible to others in textual and iconographic depictions via their recognizable patterns of dress and hair styling. The authors of the two Joseph narratives proceed with an awareness of the presence and power of such stereotypes.

In most cases, Syrian, Levantine, and Mesopotamian males are characterized by their different forms of hirsuteness. The male inhabitants of Syria and the northern Levant, from which Joseph comes, were frequently depicted having longer hair that was held at bay by a fillet or pulled back and tied. They are typically shown with full facial hair which could be trimmed to various lengths but generally covered their faces. A panel from the Black Obelisk of Shalmaneser III shows Israelites with long hair and beards bearing gifts of tribute to the Assyrian king. Likewise, the reliefs of the fall of Lachish depict Sennacherib's men leading the captives of the city off, many of whom are presented with long hair and full beards. In the same relief, other Levantine captives are depicted with shorn beards and heads, signs of emasculation and humiliation.

According to the stylized media of Egypt, the ideal Egyptian man appears to be the opposite of his northern counterpart when it came to presentations of one's hair. Men of lower social status tend to be depicted with hair on their heads but typically have clean shaven faces. The scribe pictured below, with a clean-shaven face and body, may bear resemblance to the literary depiction of Joseph as a reinstated courtier as he prepares to meet the Pharaoh (Figure 1).

Egyptian elites, on the other hand, are typically depicted as completely hairless. When they do have hair, it is a wig or a ceremonial slender beard, but no body hair (Anthony, 2017).[1] It is possible that some Pharaohs maintained heads of shorter hair under their wigs, as is evidenced by the

---

[1] This ceremonial beard was even worn by Hatshepsut, the only female leader of Egypt that we have record of.

mummy of Ramesses II (Figure 2).

Figure 1. Egyptian Scribe – Saqarra, Egypt.

The Louvre, Paris – City University of New York, 2006.

Figure 2. Bust of Ramesses II, "The Younger Memnon"

The British Museum, London.

These artistic representations have been bolstered by archaeological evidence that includes large numbers of razors in Old, Middle, and New Kingdom Egypt (Figure 3).

Figure 3. New Kingdom Razor

University College London, 2002 – Petrie, 1927

While presentations of hairless leaders are the norm in Egypt, they stand in contrast to those of Assyrian and Babylonian kings whose reliefs show their stylized but natural flowing locks and full beards as markers of their masculinity and authority (Figure 4).

Figure 4. Assurbanipal II Fighting Lions

The British Museum, London. Photo: Osama S.M. Amin.

Egyptian depictions of foreigners build on these stereotypical contrasts. The totality of artistic representations of "non-Egyptians" in ancient Egypt are far too numerous to be comprehensively accounted for here. Instead, I discuss several pertinent examples, recognizing with Phyllis Saretta, a leading expert in Egyptian iconography, that the style and contents of Egyptian iconography changed slightly over time as interconnection between Egypt and the outside world increased (Saretta, 2017). Even with diachronic changes in artistic style, several modes of visual differentiation between Egyptians and non-Egyptians remained constant, including, depictions of skin color, clothing, hairstyles, and beards.

The tomb of the Egyptian Menkheperresoneb has a painting of Syrian men bringing tribute to the Tutmosis III. Some of the men have long hair and others short. All of the Syrians are depicted with beards (Liverani, 2013 [fig. 19.4]). Additionally, a painting of the arrival of Levantine ships to Egypt depicts the sailors who likely come from Byblos or Phoenicia with long hair and full beards while the Egyptian stevedores are beardless (Davies and Faulkner, 1947 [pl. vii]). One of the most famous tomb scenes from ancient Egypt is that of the Middle Kingdom tomb complex of Khnumhotep II at Beni Hasan, where Asiatic men are portrayed in remarkable detail with the same identifying motifs of Levantine identity as they engage in a peaceful trade relationship with Egyptians. In this piece of art, the Syrian men are depicted with beards while the Egyptians have mostly shaven faces with short goatees (Figure 5).

Figure 5. Panel of Tomb Painting from Beni Hasan, Egypt

Pharaohs were tasked with the roles conquering chaos (*isfet*) and maintaining order (*ma'at*) in the earthly realms, a job which included population regulation and the subjugation of potential enemies. Thus, throughout Egyptian iconography, foreigners, including mobile populations, are typically represented in settings of subjugation (Poo, 2005). The Joseph story maintains the Egyptian disdain for pastoralists when Joseph informs his brothers that "all shepherds are abhorrent to the Egyptians" (Gen 36:34). Non-Egyptians are portrayed in text and image as wild beasts, and typically hairy in nature. They are shown being attacked, bound, in kneeling positions, and set on forced marches (Saretta, 2017). In these images, the enemies of Pharaoh are usually held by their characteristically long hair (Figure 6).

Figure 6. Ramesses III Smiting Foreigners while Holding Them by Their Hair – Abu Simbel, Egypt.

Bas relief preserved in painting by Giuseppe Angelelli, 1832.

Moreover, the physical locations where depictions of foreigners are found is telling of Egyptian dispositions toward them. Artistic representations of foreigners are frequently located on door sockets and footstools, and even on the soles of the Pharaoh's sandals as indications that they are "under the feet" of their Egyptian counterparts (Saretta, 2017).

Figure 7. Tutankhamun's Ceremonial Footstool with Bound Foreigners

Bridgeman Art Library

The typology of hairless Egyptians that are distrustful of migrant populations extends beyond iconography and into literary depictions. Though less well-known than the biblical Joseph narrative, the tale of *Sinuhe* is an Egyptian Middle Kingdom narrative and thus, a precursor to the Joseph story. The story was most likely originally a tomb autobiography and contains the account of a courtier's hastily-made escape from Egypt (Hollis, 2009). Sinuhe, fears that upon the death of King Sehetepibre (Amenemhet I) some ill will befall him before the Pharaoh's son (Senwosret I) assumes the throne. He leaves no time for his suspicions to be confirmed and makes a stealthy departure from Egypt to flee north to Levantine lands. His escape becomes an almost lifelong relocation to Syrian lands.

Towards the end of his life, Sinuhe receives a mandate from Senwosret I to return to Egypt where he shall live out the rest of his days and be properly buried. Even though he maintains that his Egyptian identity has not diminished, time passed in the lands beyond Egypt has influenced his cultural dispositions in ways apparent to Egyptians. His means of self-presentation has changed enough that it requires comment by the Pharaoh himself, who announces Sinuhe's return to the royal household by proclaiming, "Here is Sinuhe, come as an Asiatic, a product of nomads!" (Lichtheim, 2003). Perhaps it was a particular hirsuteness atypical for Egyptians that inspired such comment. Sinuhe subsequently undergoes the quintessential cosmetic treatments to restore his Egyptian-ness, among which was shaving his body.

Working at the intersections of biblical studies and the cognitive science of religion, Isaac Alderman has shown that death anxiety is deeply connected to human perceptions of animality (Alderman, 2019). Across time and geographies, humans have associated hair, particularly excess body hair, with animality. This association has not always been negative, but as we have seen, practices of limiting or removing body hair are widespread across the human experience early on. Alderman's research indicates that humans may remove hair in order to separate ourselves, even unconsciously, from other animals due to the death anxiety that is produced by recognizing our finite animal selves. His methodology is applicable to both biblical and extra-biblical sources. We can see that certain trans-human notions of disgust and animality are similarly at play in Egyptian iconography as the clean-shaven Pharaoh destroys the hairy foreigners. Furthermore, Alderman's theory of animality and death anxiety accords particularly well with Egyptian attentiveness to the afterlife.

Although iconographic evidence regarding personal hairstyles is minimal in ancient Israel, hair bears significant meaning throughout biblical literature, particularly descriptions of its removal. In the ancestral narratives, Joseph's great uncle, Esau, is the ancestor of the Edomites, a Semitic people that neighbored Israel to the southeast. Esau is identified geographically with the region of Seir/Edom, a land with nomadic peoples. The biblical descriptions of Esau highlight his hairy (Heb. *se'ar*) appearance and may demonstrate that Semitic peoples maintained their own set of criteria for acceptable levels of hairiness since Esau's hirsuteness was associated with his brash nature as a nomadic hunter and warrior (Gen 25, 22-28).

According to legal texts in the Pentateuch, the presentation of one's hair was of import to the community for both hygienic and religious reasons. In the case of lepers, straggly and sullied hair and beards are a sign of their ritual uncleanliness. The shaving of both after being cured of an ailment is a sign to the community that a man has been restored to proper standing (Lev,13-14). Likewise, shaving and nail-trimming is part of a ritual for inducting captive foreign women into the covenant community where they can become potential wives (Deut, 21:12).

By and large, the multiple occurrences of hair removal in the Hebrew Bible bear negative connotations. In Israelite folklore, the story of Samson conveys that his abundant locks perform dual duty as the symbol of his Nazarite vows and source of his strength. Samson's subsequent demise turns on the moment when Delilah has a barber shave his hair (Heb. *wattᵉgallaḥ / gullaḥ*), leading to his capture by the Philistines (Jdgs, 16:17-22; cf. Num 6:5, 18). In a later biblical account, David's son Absalom meets his end when his long hair is caught in an oak tree (2 Sam 19). Drawing on the idea that hair symbolizes power, this historiographical episode may intimate the notion that Absalom's power and misuse of it was the reason for his own demise. Other instances of hair cutting are associated with military conquest and capture. The mirrored accounts of two Samuel 10:4 and 1 Chronicles 19:4 tell of Hunan's capture of David's men, whereby in addition to cutting their garments, he further humiliates them by having half of each man's beard shaved.

The tropes of humiliation and punishment are further drawn out through the prophetic critiques of Israel and Judah's covenantal ruptures, which biblical authors see as the cause of Israel and Judah's destruction by eastern imperial powers. Throughout these texts, the terminology of shaving carries greater semantic freight than simple hair removal. The orthographically and phonetically similar terms for shaving (*glḥ* / גלח) and exile (*glḥ* / גלה) are used interchangeably as real and metaphorical indicators of Israel and Judah's experiences of suffering and destruction. It is at this juncture of shaving and exile that the concerns of the Hebrew authors responsible for the Joseph text come into clear sight.

Speaking to the leaders of the northern kingdom, the prophet Amos relays the divine message that God will "bring baldness (Heb. *qorḥa*) on every head" (Amos 8:10). Later, Isaiah proclaims God's impending action of "shaving" (Heb. *yᵉgallaḥ*) Israel through the actions of the Assyrian king (Isa 7:20) as God's hired "razor" (Heb. *ṭaʿar*). Moreover, Isaiah's son bears the name, *Shear-Yashub*, meaning, "a remnant will return." The sign act of naming his child this is a prophetic pronouncement of divine salvation from endless exile and plays, like the naming of Esau, on the language of "hair" (Heb. *se'ar*) with "remnant" (Heb. *she'ar*).

Ezekiel, a forced migrant and prophet, employs the image of hair cutting as a means to speak about destruction through exile. He pushes the bounds of eccentricity in his enactment of the depilation metaphor whereby through the removal, distribution, and destruction of portions of his hair and beard, he makes known God's word that Jerusalem will be punished for their recalcitrance (Ezk 5:1-4). Ezekiel's behavior is not without an antecedent. In various parts of the ancient Near East, hair was conceived of in magical terms and as an attendant element of religious praxis. It was common for prophets and prophetesses to send a clipping of their own hair and a fragment torn from the hem of their garment as seals of the veracity of their divinatory proclamations (Nissinen, 2003).

Finally, the self-removal of hair as a public signal of mourning is also found throughout the biblical record. Following the fall of Samaria, Micah calls the people of Israel to make themselves bald (Heb. qorḥi) in suffering response to their own children's deportation to Assyria (Mic, 1:16). Jeremiah records the moment when offering-bearers from Shechem, Shiloh, and Samaria come with their beards shaved (Heb. mᵉgullᵉhe) in mourning to offer sacrifice in the ransacked region of Jerusalem (Jer, 41:5). In the same way, Ezra responds to the intermarriage of returned exiles with the peoples of the Land by forcefully rubbing the hair from his head and beard (Ezra, 9:3). Interestingly, these depilating behaviors are not uniformly condoned by the biblical authors. Thus, the legal texts of Leviticus 19:27 and 21:5 forbid the cutting of one's beard or purposeful mangling of one's hair as acts of mourning.

Recognizing that presentations and removal of one's hair bears such import throughout the biblical record, one cannot simply pass over the mention of Joseph's shaving in Genesis 41:14. Though brief, the mention of Joseph's actions is momentous. I argue that the authors who inherited and translated the Hebrew form of the text into Greek were attentive to the importance of this plot element and engaged it in a way that presented their own assertions regarding acculturation.

Acculturation and Integration through Image-Changing

With the historical and linguistic contexts of the Joseph story illuminated, readers can recognize that more is at stake in the telling of this tale than the story of a forced migrant who finds success in the land of his captors. The story's proclamations about divine protection, redemption, and future suffering are wrapped up with profound questions about the nature and extent of identity negotiation in foreign contexts. Moreover, when one compares the Greek and Hebrew forms of the story, we find a lively conversation about ethnic and religious boundary preservation through which different communities are working to answer questions such as: How is the *Self* reconstituted in the absence of a home community? What are the acceptable limits of cultural adaptation/assimilation? Which elements of culture/society can be manipulated (either through accentuation or erasure) to encourage flourishing? In recognizing this, readers can proceed with the a hermeneutic that attends to the complexity of identity-crises faced by migrants and the internal social commentary that groups offer on the spectrum of migrants' assimilative choices.

The corpus of literature on social and cultural assimilation is vast. Moreover, the terminology of assimilation is contested ground since, "[I]n recent decades assimilation has come to be viewed by social scientists as a worn-out theory which imposes ethnocentric and patronizing demands on minority peoples struggling to retain their cultural and ethnic integrity" (Alba & Nee, 1997, Cf. Fitzgerald, 2015). This claim maintains an additional level of truth in the contexts of forced migration where individuals have decreased agency and any impetus to adapt might come more from a place of need than want. Yet, even with this salient critique, Richard Alba and Victor Nee maintain that assimilation as a "social science concept" is useful and should be retained but reformulated. I concur that a nuanced understanding of assimilation can address processes of cultural interface, and thus I apply it going forward to the investigation of Joseph's acculturative behaviors (Cf. Glazer, 1993; Morawska, 1994; Nagel, 2009).

In addition to Alba and Nee's contributions, the present discussion of assimilation and media is informed by John Berry's model of acculturation attitudes, in which assimilation is but one outcome. Berry's work has been widely accepted among scholars attempting to understand processes of socio-cultural maintenance and change across the spectrum of cultural contact (Berry, 1980; Berry et al., 1987; Alba and Foner, 2015, Berry, 2019). According to Berry and his various co-authors, individuals who are willing to relinquish major elements of previous cultural identities and accept new traits are seen as participants in *assimilation*. In this process, one's first culture takes a back seat to the demands of adaptation for reasons that can range from survival to preference. Those who adopt new traits while simultaneously maintaining elements of their previous identities are described as participants in *integration*. This second category of adaptive behavior is often seen as the ideal for migrants but is in reality a difficult place to be as the tension between one's first and second cultures can foment into ruptured ties between important individuals and institutions on both sides of the cultural divide. Such questions regarding the boundaries of integrative behavior are at the core of the Joseph story. Moreover, when the discrepancies between the

Hebrew and Greek versions are attended to, we see that distinct authorial and receiving communities answer these questions differently.

Berry's third category, *separation*, is the result of a positive answer to the question of maintaining home cultural traits while answering negatively to the adoption of new elements. This pattern of behavior commonly results in persons maintaining the status of foreigner or Other in new social context. Their ability to flourish as such is then tied to the society's elasticity for accommodating difference. Finally, the fourth category of acculturation, *marginalization,* is defined by a doubly-negative answer to the questions of cultural relinquishment and cultural adoption. Individuals who do not maintain their home culture and who do not attempt to adopt or adapt to secondary cultural elements risk becoming unaligned from both cultural contexts and in a dangerous cultural no-mans-land (Berry, 1980; Berry et al., 1987).

Berry's work illuminates the reality that acculturation is processual and occurs along both group and individual axes. Rarely, if ever, are processes of assimilation or acculturation unidirectional. Processes of negotiation take place between a migrant's personal identity, meaning those goals, values, assumptions closest to the person, and one's social identity, meaning those larger contexts of group behaviors, cultural repertoires, and belonging (Schwartz, Montgomery, and Briones, 2006). Moreover, while the pressures of a dominant or majority culture can be overwhelming, the process of assimilation does not always lead to the erasure of ethnic identity.

It is important that Berry's categories are not interpreted as static, but rather as points along a continuum of ongoing acculturative responses that depend on the cultural trait(s) in question (Ward, 2013; Ward and Geeraert, 2016). In accordance with growing understandings of the nature of the human self as a dialogical and multi-dimensional agent, the acculturative rubric must represent the realities that individual cultural negotiation is more complex than rote exchange between discreet cultural identities (O'Sullivan-Lago and de Abreu, 2010). This is especially true as scholarship continues to mount persuasive presentations regarding biculturalism and multiple-identity embeddedness as modes of migrant interaction in diverse cultural contexts (Ozyurt, 2013; Chams, 2015; Compton-Lilly et al., 2017). Insomuch, the kinds of acculturative moves that a forced migrant like Joseph makes are not determined merely by the desire to maintain or obtain cultural attributes. Social, economic, and environmental forces beyond his control influence both the range of available acculturative choices and one's capacities to act on them.

Though the variables influencing responses to migrants are many, migrants are often the target of critiques on their appearance. There are strong correlations between migrants' visible cultural adaptation and their treatment by larger society, as well as direct links between racial perceptions and the treatment of migrants (Hersch, 2011). Kunst, et al. demonstrate that immigrants with lighter skin are perceived as being more willing to assimilate to dominant American culture. Furthermore, they show that Americans are more likely to consider immigrants who readily adopt visible elements of American popular culture as racially White (Kunst, Dovidio, and Dotsch, 2018; See also Byrne and Dixon, 2016). These findings accord well with Egyptian literature explored above that refers to non-Egyptians in derogatory ways and propagates fears that Semitic/Asiatic, and sea-borne invaders are going to destroy the country.

Across the spectrum, migrants show a remarkable awareness of the appearances most associated with dominant groups in a given society (Garćia, 2014; Ybarra, 2019). Responses to such recognitions differ considerably. What is clear is that migrants' bodies are "contested terrain" where notions of *Self* and *Other* are reified (Kraut, 2014). Identity negotiation is both purposeful and strategic. Likewise, it depends on the various forms of capital, including social capital, that one possesses in a particular environment. Maria Lidola's research demonstrates how body image and hair removal can take center stage in the integration process (Lidola, 2014). While the research provides little assistance for generating any predictive patterns of behavior, the overall picture is one in which migrants do what is expedient and effective given their agency in their present social structures and the available means for change within their new context. Understanding the tensions that arise through these context-specific processes of negotiation can help us better understand the variant stances taken by both the authors and translators of the Joseph narrative.

The centrality of these texts in the communities from which they come cannot be overstated. The Jacob-Joseph narratives of Genesis are foundational accounts of ancestral origins for several communities dispersed across geographies. Nevertheless, the interpretation and further shaping of those accounts by each community varies. Both texts are characteristically terse in nature and possess narrative gaps that the reader must fill in. In addition, the intention of Joseph's assimilative behavior is not clearly stated in either. It is clear, though, that one authorial community maintains a stronger position of resistance to assimilation, even in contexts of forced migration, than an another. In the Hebrew account, Joseph's behavior appears to be willful integration. In the Greek version, he is the victim of forced identity transformation. The change in the locus of agency is significant for what it conveys about the authorial communities responsible for the final forms of the texts.

The Hebrew authors build a case against Joseph throughout the narrative by which readers find Joseph's adaptive strategies tending toward integration as he responds pragmatically to his experience. Shaving is only one element of his assimilation. He also learns to speak Egyptian, takes on the Egyptian name, marries an Egyptian woman who is the daughter of an Egyptian priest (41:45), and adopts Egyptian foodways. Yet, while he is willing to adopt certain Egyptian characteristics mentioned above, he maintains distinct and significant elements of his home cultural identity. As an example, he gives his two sons Hebrew names, even though they are born into the Egyptian noble class. Such onomastic activity can be read as instructive for migrant behavior in a foreign land, as one's name can mark cultural affiliations, even when the named individual is native to the foreign place (Aceto, 2002; Arai and Thoursie, 2009; Spitzer, 2010; Khosravi, 2012). Such is the case for Joseph's children. The translators of the Greek give similar accounts of Joseph's subsequent assimilative behaviors, though, the critique does not register as sharply because following his shaving, it appears to readers that Joseph either had no choice in these other matters or was wise in opting to become more Egyptian.

The differences between the two versions appear in stark contrast again as the narrative recounts the end of Jacob and Joseph's lives. Jacob and Joseph separately desire that their bones will be carried to the land of Canaan following their deaths. Many migrants, forced and voluntary alike, hope to return to their homeland, even if only in their death, for there is great tragedy in being laid to rest in a place that is not one's home.[2] At this point of the narrative, the Hebrew version preserves another critique of Joseph's assimilative choices. Jacob's explicit request is to be taken back to his ancestors, which Joseph promises, but only does after embalming his father in the Egyptian style. The same is true for Joseph at the end of his life, who is also embalmed in the Hebrew version. This is, in many ways, a final act of body modification. In doing so, Joseph is forever preserving his Egyptianized identity, and extending it to his father. One can imagine the oddity of Jacob and Joseph's embalmed bodies being laid to rest in a typical family-style secondary inhumation tomb where only the bones of his ancestors lay.

The Hebrew and Greek authors again deal differently with this acculturative episode. While, the Hebrew text uses the term for embalming (חנט), the Greek translators opt for a word that simply means to prepare a body for burial (ἐνταφιάζω). Their choice is deliberate, as there would have been contemporary terms that specifically indicated embalming. They simply do not use them. The reason for this is ultimately unclear. I venture two potential reasons: First, it may be that they amend the story because they

---

[2] The notion of migrant return is attended by a complex discussion of definitions, central to which is the contested meaning of "home." For a range of perspectives on the issue, see Toren, 1976; Parutis, 2014; Datta, 2017).

don't want to show that Joseph would willingly become so Egyptian as to take on their notions about the afterlife. Secondly, perhaps members of their community have begun practicing similar burial rites and they wish to downplay the difference between their ancestral practices and their own.

At the center of the different presentations of Joseph's experience are variant collective memories of Egypt, the hegemon that looms large in the background of many of the ancestral narratives. More than any other location or empire in the Bible, Egypt is a place of complex relational tensions for Israel's ancestors and the covenant community. On one hand, according to the biblical authors, Egypt is land of plenty. Its riverine empire is the bread basket of the ancient Near East that provides food for the climatic and agriculturally marginal zones of the Levant. Genesis relays the historical realities of pastoralist populations that depended on Egyptian foodstuffs in times of regional famine. On the other hand, Egypt is a land of slavery, of intense xenophobia, and of brutal conquest. The fundamental story of Israel's existence, its national narrative of the Exodus from Egypt, tells of a people's divinely-orchestrated escape from the grip of enslavement and the power of their God, Yahweh, over the gods of Egypt and the Pharaoh. The Joseph narrative, though likely a story that is chronologically more recent in its origins than the Exodus account, sets the stage for biblical readers by providing an explanation of how the Hebrew people ended up in Egypt and in need of saving in the first place. When one reads the Joseph story, they likely do so with these tensions in mind, aware of the fact that at various points in Israel's history, Egypt was both savior and oppressor.

The authors of the Hebrew version of the narrative are far removed from the geographic contexts of enslavement in Egypt. Yet, they face the realities of life as a minority under imperial rule. Their daily lives are filled with identity negotiations and the desire to maintain a sense of self and people. Thus, the Judahite authors of the Hebrew version lean further toward *separation* than their Greek-speaking counterparts. Their concerns for ethnic preservation are rooted in notions of religious purity and the proper maintenance of their covenantal relationship with God.

Living at a later period than the Hebrew authors and seasoned by more than a century of relative safety and prosperity in Egypt, the Greek authors concerns are less calcified. Ultimately, the narrative of a Hebrew-made-Egyptian is probably less threatening to them. Even more, the story of Hebrews escaping their Egyptian oppressors that follows the Joseph narrative in the Pentateuch likely has a very different ring, since the memories of oppressive Pharaohs or enslavement in Egypt have become part of the distant past. These different collective memories of Egyptian hegemony result in their integration with Egyptian society and a divergent Joseph story.

Seeing Joseph in Relationship to other Biblical Media

It would be difficult to identify the Hebrew authors' critiques of Joseph if the story was an isolated account. As it stands, however, it is part of a broader corpus of migration-informed texts in the Hebrew Bible. Like the prophet Jeremiah's admonitions to those in exiled in Babylon to "Seek the peace of the city" (Jer. 29:7), the account of Joseph's life portrays an instance in which a Hebrew migrant could positively impact the circumstances of a foreign empire as a means of self-preservation. Indeed, according to the narrative, Egypt benefits greatly from Joseph's lifetime of loyal service to Pharaoh. Moreover, Joseph manages to sustain his family's life and thus secures the future of a people. Yet, while the outcomes of his actions are praiseworthy in one regard, there is also an inherent problematizing of their long-term effects. Joseph's deeds save his family and many Egyptians, but, by the end the story, they ultimately lead to the enslavement of his descendants and to that of other landless Egyptians.

The biblical authors maintain the key theological momentum of the narrative, which is that Israel's God is present with Joseph as a forced migrant and works to ensure the future of a people. Other key figures in the biblical text, like Israel's kings Saul, David, and Solomon, are both praised and critiqued by the biblical authors. Joseph, as a central character in Israel's past, cannot escape the same double-edge sword. Just as Solomon's life become instructive of the nature of wisdom and his inability to live fully into it, Joseph's life becomes instructive for all the members of the covenant community faced with the challenges of negotiating their identity in the contexts of exile, diaspora, or foreign ruler-ship. We can compare the presentation of Joseph's experience to that of other narratives about migrants and Hebrews in foreign courts. The story of Daniel, another exiled Israelite, offers a clear picture of the assimilation strategy preferred by the final redactors of the Hebrew Joseph account.

As a Judean captive in Babylon, Daniel's story mirrors many elements of Joseph's experience in Egypt (Dan 1-2, 4-6). His rise to success through dream interpretation plays on a similar motif. Moreover, Daniel is portrayed as an exceedingly wise agent of God and counselor capable of influencing the mind of the ruler of a foreign land. Like Joseph, he and his compatriots learn the language, literature and law of their captors. Yet, several elements of the narrative about Daniel stand in stark contrast to Joseph. Daniel maintains Israelite dietary restrictions that have become so important as group identifiers in Exile. The implied historical setting of the Joseph account predates that of the stories about Daniel and thus understandably do not include the concerns for keeping Kosher food practices. Nevertheless, the fact remains that Joseph refuses to eat with his brothers, because it would break Egyptian customs of sharing a table with foreigners. Most importantly,

Daniel rejects the gifts of clothing and adornment from the king Belshazzar while also rebuking him for being haughty. In this way, Daniel appears as the Hebrew in exile *par excellence*. He is capable rising to unparalleled success while also maintaining his distinctive identity as an Israelite worshiper of God.

These different narratives which are contained in the same religious text show that the communities responsible for their authorship and reception existed in different geographic contexts, experienced different historical realities, and maintained different perspectives on the proper responses of those who proclaimed to be members of the Israelite covenant community to the questions that these narratives pose. We have seen that the Hebrew and Greek versions of the Joseph story do not answer these challenges univocally. The striking thing about these ancient forms of media, is not only that bear witness to socio-religious conversations about forced migration, assimilation, acculturation, and body modification, but that they have been intentionally preserved in the same collection of religious texts where they stand simultaneously in complementary and contrastive juxtaposition to one another.

Conclusion

Both the Hebrew and Greek forms of the Joseph story display authorial awareness of the cultural norms of Egyptian shaving preserved in a wide variety of Egyptian media. In them, we see that two communities, separated by geography and time, and having undergone dissimilar migrational experiences, cultivate unique media responses to the assimilative challenges before them in the form of body modification.

We have seen that a literary creation like the Joseph story can reveal a great deal about the authors responsible for their production and the audience(s) intended for their reception. These ancient narratives also convey the ever-present reality that different forms of migration-informed media can be set in dialogue with one another to better understand their origins and differences, but also to gain perspective on our own experiences with migration today. Textual and iconographic portrayals of migrant populations have purchase on the way migrants see themselves as well as the ways others see them. Beyond informing perceptions, these depictions can prompt a range of positive and negative responses to migrant persons. Insofar, these texts had and have the power to both perpetuate and challenge stereotypes. Likewise, they have been and can be used to substantiate claims of ethnic boundaries and establish ethical protocols for dealing with perceived deviant persons or groups who break assimilative norms.

Finally, each of the forms of media discussed in this chapter can be approached as resources by both migrants and scholars of migration. Careful and informed readings of them can make us aware of our own prejudices and predispositions. They can provide spaces to discuss the difficult questions regarding assimilation, integration, and broader concerns among both migrants and receiving societies about identity negotiation. With their many facets, they can function as mirrors for our own times as we work to understand migrants and migration in the past and present.

References

Aceto, M. (2002). "Ethnic Personal Names and Multiple Identities in Anglophone Caribbean Speech Communities in Latin America. Language in Society, 31(4), 577-608.

Alba, R., & Foner, N. (2015). Strangers No More: Immigration and the Challenges of Integration in North America and Western Europe. Princeton, NJ: Princeton University Press.

Alba, R., & Nee, V. (1997). Rethinking Assimilation Theory for a New Era of Immigration. The International Migration Review, 31(4), 825-874.

Alderman, I. M. (2019). The Animal at Unease with Itself: Death Anxiety and the Human-Animal Boundary in Genesis 2-3. Lexington, KY: Fortress Academic.

Anthony, F. B. (2017). Foreigners in Ancient Egypt: Theban Tomb Paintings from the Early Eighteenth Dynasty (Bloomsbury Egyptology). London: Bloomsbury Academic.

Arai, M., & Thoursie, P. S. (2009). Renouncing Personal Names: An Empirical Examination of Surname Change and Earnings. Journal of Labor and Economics, 27(1), 127-147.

Berry, J. W., Kim, U., Minde, T., & Mok, D. (1987). Comparative Models of Acculturative Stress. The International Migration Review, 21(3), 491-511.

Berry, J.W. (2019). Acculturation: A Personal Journey Across Cultures. Cambridge, Cambridge University Press.

Byrne, J., & Dixon, G. C. (2016). Just Not Like Us: The Interactive Impact of Dimensions of Identity and Race in Attitudes towards Immigration. Social Sciences, 5(59). doi:10.3390/socsci5040059

Chams, W. (2015). Living in a Transnational World: Identity Negotiation and Formation among Second Generation Lebanese Young Adults Living in London Ontario (Unpublished master's thesis). Western University. Retrieved from http://ir.lib.uwo.ca/sociology_masrp/2

Compton-Lilly, C., Papoi, K., Venegas, P., Hamman, L., & Schwabenbauer, B. (2017). Intersectional Identity Negotiation: The Case of Young Immigrant Children. Journal of Literacy Research,49(1), 115-140.

Datta, A. (2017). Uncertain Journeys: Return Migration, Home, and Uncertainty for a Displaced Kashmiri Community. Modern Asian Studies, 51(4), 1099-1125.

Davies, N. D., & Faulkner, R. O. (1947). A Syrian Trading Venture to Egypt. Journal of Egyptian Archaeology, 33, 40-46.

Dines, J. (2004). The Septuagint. London: T & T Clark.

Evans, J., & Withey, A. (Eds.). (2018). New Perspectives on the History of Facial Hair: Framing the Face (Genders and Sexualities in History). Cham, CH: Palgrave Macmillan - Springer.

Fernandez, A. A., França, K., Chacon, A. H., & Nouri, K. (2013). From Flint Razors to Lasers: A Timeline of Hair Removal Methods. Journal of Cosmetic Dermatology, 12(2), 153-162. doi:10.1111/jocd.12021

Fitzgerald, D. S. (2015). The Sociology of International Migration. In C. B. Brettel & J. F. Hollifield (Eds.), Migration Theory: Talking Across Disciplines (3rd ed., pp. 115-147).

London: Routledge the Reinscribing of Tradition. Cambridge: Cambridge University Press.

Garćia, A. (2014). Hidden in Plain Sight: How Unauthorised Migrants Strategically Assimilate in Restrictive Localities in California. Journal of Ethnic and Migration Studies, 40(12), 1895-1914.

Glazer, N. (1993). Is Assimilation Dead. The Annals of the American Academy of Social and Political Sciences, 530, 122-136.

Hersch, J. (2011). The Persistence of Skin Color Discrimination for Immigrants. Social Science Research, 40, 1337-1349.

Fleming, D. E. (2012). The Legacy of Israel in Judah's Bible: History, Politics, and

Hollis, S. T. (2009). Egyptian Literature. In C. S. Ehrlich (Ed.), From an Antique Land: An Introduction to Ancient Near Eastern Literature (pp. 77-136). Lanham: Rowman & Littlefield.

Khosravi, S. (2012). White Masks/Muslim Names: Immigrants and Name-Changing in Sweeden. Race and Class, 53(3), 65-80.

Kirchoff, M. and Kitson, N. (2013). Trends in Body Hair Removal as Depicted through Art. Journal of the American Academy of Dermatology, 68, AB34.

Kraut, A. M. (2014). Doing as Americans Do: The Post-Migration Negotiation of Identity in the United States. The Journal of American History, 101(3), 707-725.

Kunst, J. R., Dovidio, J. F., & Dotsch, R. (2018). White Look-Alike: Mainstream Cultural Adoption Makes Immigrants 'Look' Phenotypically White. Personality and Social Psychology Bulletin, 44(2), 265-282.

Lichtheim, M. (2003). Sinuhe. In W. W. Hallo & K. L. Younger (Eds.), The Context of Scripture: Canonical Compositions from the Biblical World (Vol. 1, Contexts of Scripture, pp. 77-82). Leiden, ND: Brill.

Lidola, M. (2014). Negotiating Integration in Berlin's Waxing Studios: Brazilian Migrants' Gendered Appropriation of Urban Consumer Spaces and 'Ethnic' Entrepreneurship. Journal of Contemporary History, 49(1), 228-251.

Liverani, M. (2013). S. Tabatai (trans.), The Ancient Near East: History, Society, and Economy. London: Routledge.

Morawska, E. (1994). In Defense of the Assimilation Model. Journal of American Ethnic History, 13, 76-87.

Nagel, C. R. (2009). Rethinking Geographies of Assimilation. The Professional Geographer, 61(3), 400-407.

Nissinen, M. (2003). Prophets and Prophecy in the Ancient Near East (Vol. 12, Writings from the Ancient World). Atlanta, GA: Society of Biblical Literature.

O'Sullivan, R., & De Abreu, G. (2010). Maintaining Continuity in a Cultural Contact Zone: Identification Strategies in the Dialogical Self. Culture & Psychology, 16(1), 73-92.

Ozyurt, S. (2013). Negotiating Multiple Identities: Constructing Wester-Muslim Selves in the Netherlands and the United States. Political Psychology,34(2), 239-263.

Parutis, V. (2014). Returning 'Home': East European Migrants' Discourses of Return. International Migration, 52(5), 159-177.

Poo, Mu-Chu. (2005). Enemies of Civilization: Attitudes towards Foreigners in Ancient Mesopotamia, Egypt, and China Albany, State University of New York Press.

Saretta, P. (2017). Asiatics in Middle Kingdom Egypt (Bloomsbury Egyptology). London: Bloomsbury Academic.

Schipper, B. U. (2018). Joseph, Ahiqar, and Elephantine: The Joseph Story as a Diaspora Novella. Journal of Ancient Egyptian Interconnections, 18, 71-84.

Schwartz, S., Montgomery, M., & Briones, E. (2006). The Role of Identity in Acculturation among Immigrant People: Theoretical Propositions, Empirical Questions, and Applied Recommendations. Human Development, 49(1), 1-30.

Spitzer, L. (2010). A Name Given, A Name Taken: Camouflaging, Resistance, and Diasporic Social Identity. Comparative Studies of South Asia, Africa, and the Middle

East, 30(1), 21-31.

Toren, T. (1976). Return to Zion: Characteristics and Motivations of Returning Emigrants. Social Forces, 54, 546-558.

Van De Mieroop, M. (2016). A History of the Ancient Near East (3rd ed.). Malden, MA: Wiley Blackwell.

Ward, C. (2013). Probing Identity, Integration and Adaptation: Big Questions, Little Answers. International Journal of Intercultural Relations, 37, 391-404.

Ward, C., & Geeraert, N. (2016). Advancing acculturation theory and research: The acculturation process in its ecological context. Current Opinion in Psychology, 8, 98-104.

Ybarra, M. (2019). "We are not ignorant": Transnational Migrants' Experiences of Racialized Securitization. Society and Space,37(2), 197-215.

CHAPTER 5

'THE NEW DIASPORA' AND INTERACTIVE MEDIA CAMPAIGNS: THE CASE OF ROMANIANS MIGRATING TO THE UK AFTER BREXIT

Bianca Florentina Cheregi

A few days after the United Kingdom voted for Brexit, the Romanian newspaper *Gândul* and the advertising agency *Webstyler* has launched the "Romanians Adopt Remainians" campaign. The initiative has encouraged Romanians to reach out to the 16 million Britons who voted to remain in the European Union and symbolically adopt them. In this regard, the *Gândul* website targets the Britons who believe in a united Europe and tells them to "leave the Brexiters, the quarrelling and the weather behind" in order to start "a new life in a loving Romanian family" (Romanians Adopt Remainians, 2016). As we can see, the Romanian journalists are actively involving the citizens in the public debate, by initiating interactive media campaigns.

In Romania, the topic of labor migration to the EU "the new diaspora" is constantly approached by the media, sometimes involving intense *mediatisation* (Couldry & Hepp, 2013; Livingstone, 2009; Lundby, 2014), depending on social and political contexts such as the as the 2010 crisis about the Romani people's expulsion from France back to Romania and Bulgaria, the economic crisis, Romania's accession to the Schengen Area, the freedom of movement in the EU, and therefore in the UK (Cheregi, 2018, 20) or, more recently, the Brexit vote. The Brexit and the current state of affairs in Europe (mainly the rise of the right-wing nationalist parties such as the UK Independence Party – UKIP – and The National Front in France) force us to rethink the basis of transnational migration and whether these impacts both the individual and the society.

In the contemporary "age of migration" (Castles & Miller, 2003), people develop transnational identities by travelling between different locations. A special case is that of Romanian people migrating to the UK, generating a debate in the British and Romanian media as well. Moreover, the journalists provide their own definitions and interpretations of migration, considering the intensification of discourses on the topic of Romanian migration in the British press.

Media discourses activate modes of engagement at a distance and provide resources for the articulation of cultural and political belonging to various communities (national, local and diasporic), fashioning themselves as sites of symbolic power (Beciu et al., 2017). In the particular case of Romania, the diaspora is seen as "the result of massive migration occurring after the fall of communism, be it the migration of the unskilled labor force, benefiting preeminence both in media and public debates, or the migration of highly-skilled professionals" (Ciocea & Cârlan, 2012, p.184). For Ragazzi (as cited in Brunnbauer, 2010), "diaspora" is a word of politics: a linguistic and social construction that serves a particular purpose.

On the January 1, 2014, the restrictions limiting the access of Romanian and Bulgarian citizens to the job market in the EU, including the United Kingdom, were lifted. A year before, the British Government launched the *Don't Come to Britain!* campaign, spurring a debate about migration. The Romanian media responded with the *Why don't you come over?* campaign (*Gândul*, January 2013), humorously dismissing the British negative portrayal of Romanians. Other campaigns responding to media discourses from the United Kingdom on the migration issue are *Let's Change the Story!* (*Gândul*, January 2014), *The Truth About Romanian People in Great Britain* (*Adevărul*, March 2014) and *Romanians in the UK* (ProTv, April 2015). In June 2016, the Romanian newspaper *Gândul* launched the "Romanians Adopt Remainians" campaign, encouraging Romanians to symbolically adopt Britons who voted to remain in the EU. Therefore, the journalists have reconfigured their role as professionals in order to assume a civic role (Couldry, 2007; Roselle, 2003; Silverstone, 2007), by engaging citizens in the public debate.

In this context, this chapter focuses on analysing the role of Romanian and British journalists in the problematization of migration, taking into account two different contexts: (1) the freedom of movement for Romanian and Bulgarian citizens to work inside the UK, starting January 1, 2014 and (2) the British referendum of June 23, 2016.

The topic of labor migration to the EU is linked to two rival paradigms, according to Boswell and Geddes (2011). One can notice a liberal, free-trade-oriented paradigm, based on the economic benefit of free movement, but also a state-centric, restrictive paradigm, revealing the impact of migration and mobility on the state's capacity to allocate socio-economic and political resources (Boswell and Geddes, 2011). The underlying assumption connected to the free movement of European citizens is that "immigration is partly driven by a desire to take advantage of generous welfare systems in destination countries" (Balch, 2018, 167). The media tend to use the social benefit frame by referring to migrants (particularly Romanian migrants) that abuse the social benefits system in the United Kingdom (NHS, housing, benefits for families, children, etc.) (Cheregi, 2018).

In the particular case of Romania, the topic of labor migration to the UK is connected to Romania's country image, one of the most controversial topics in the Romanian media over the past few years. Soon after the fall of communism in 1989, this issue became part of the public debate about the international perception of Romanian people, about the ways in which Romania is depicted in the international press, or about the country's position in the process of Europeanization (Cheregi, 2018). The theme of Romanians migrating to other countries is also connected to the debate on nation branding, and in relation to the ways in which the migrants' actions influence the country image: a key element of the "symbolic capital" of the nation (Beciu, 2012).

On the other hand, the topic of the British referendum is also connected to the public problem of Romanian migration to EU countries. In fact, according to (Hobolt, 2016), "the British leave voters were motivated by anti-immigration and anti-establishment feelings." There was a divide between those who felt left behind by the forces of globalization and those who welcomed such developments. An important fact here is that the less-well educated and the less-well-off voted to leave the EU, while the young graduates in the urban centres voted to stay (Hobolt, 2016).

Economy and immigration were the main arguments brought into attention by the media, before the EU referendum. According to one YouGov poll, 84 per cent of Leave voters thought that there would be "less immigration into Britain" if the UK left the EU, compared to only 27 per cent of Remain voters. Strong national identity (especially English identity) is associated with the Leave vote, while voters with a European identity would be more likely to vote to remain in the EU (Hobolt, 2016).

The nature of nationhood is changing in the age of globalization, marketization, and mediatization. This leads to a further discussion about the ways in which the journalists give their own interpretations to migration as a public problem, taking into account different types of communication situations. This chapter focuses both on controlled media discourses campaigns initiated by the media to respond to the anti-immigration discourses from the British tabloid press) and on meta-discourses around the campaigns. It draws on a multidisciplinary approach, combining media studies, public diplomacy, sociology, discourse analysis and semiotics.

In fact, the country image is a *public problem* (Boltanski, Cefai & Gusfield, 2001), because the Romanian journalists provide their own definitions and interpretations of the country image in different contexts, some of them explicit (such as nation branding), and some implicit (such as migration as an intensively debated theme in the public sphere) (Cheregi, 2018).

In this context, the research questions underlying this study are:

RQ1: How do the journalists define migration as a public problem, in the context of the freedom of movement to work inside the EU and the Brexit vote, comparatively?

RQ2: How do interactive media campaigns on Romanian migration construct national and collective identity discourses?

RQ3: What are the main semiotic resources employed in the campaign and how are they organized?

In order to answer these questions, the analysis covers the ways in which the campaigns represent counter-discourses, relying on forms of engagement and audience mobilization (discourses of identity), but also on the way in which journalists have built their relationship with the "other," constructing discourses of alterity.

The corpus covers five interactive mass-media campaigns on Romanian migration - *Don't Come to Britain! (The Guardian,* January 2013), *Why Don't You Come Over? (Gândul,* January 2013), *Let's Change the Story! (Gândul,* January 2014), *The Truth about Romanians Migrating to the UK (Adevărul,* March 2014) and *Romanians Adopt Remainians (Gândul,* June 2016) and 100 news articles around the campaigns.

For an in-depth analysis of mass-media campaigns on Romanian migration, a *multimodal* approach is employed, highlighting the importance of image, sound and text as semiotic resources. In this particular case, *multimodality* provides the means to describe a practice or representation in all its semiotic complexity (Iedema, 2003). Methodologically, the analysis is based on qualitative research methods, combining *multimodal* analysis (Iedema, 2003; Kress & van Leeuwen, 2006) with critical discourse analysis (Van Dijk, 1993; van Leeuwen, 2008) and *dispositif* analysis (Charaudeau, 2005; Lochard, 2005, 2006; Soulages, 2007).

The aim of this chapter is to analyse discourses and counter-discourses in the specific context of Romanians migrating to the UK. The focus is on investigating the role of Romanian journalist in constructing the public problem of migration, in two different contexts: the freedom of movement to work inside the EU and the Brexit vote.

The next two sections introduce in more detail the theoretical framework, presenting the role of the media in constructing migration as a public problem, from a sociological perspective. An overview of research in migration studies is more than necessary to understand the main paradigms and schools of thought. Then, the paper moves forward to interactive media campaigns as *dispositifs*, highlighting the importance of image, music and text in the discursive construction of migration as a public problem. The methodological tools for analysing media campaigns and meta-discourses around the campaigns are presented in-depth. Finally, the discussion insists on the findings resulting from the analysis of the five interactive media campaigns on Romanian migration, along with news discourses around them.

The role of the media in constructing migration as a public problem

In a book about politics of belonging, Yuval-Davis (2011) raises the question of the people's nationality, comparing it to religious and political beliefs. Her focus is on studying why should people feel more loyal to a nation than to other political and religious collectivites. The concept of politics of belonging describes "not only construction of boundaries but also the inclusion or exclusion of particular people, social categories and groupings within these boundaries by those who have the power to do this" (Yuval-Davis, 2011, 17). Belonging is constructed in relation to particular collectivities, which are sometimes conditioned by spatial boundaries.

The neoliberal ideology and the mobility of the globalized economy have affected nationalist political projects of belonging. Considering these facts, the diasporic and transnational belongings can transcend the limits of physical geography, especially by using the Internet. Thus, constructions of self and identity can be forced on people, constituting a field of contestation. In this case, the boundaries of the politics of belonging are the boundaries which "sometimes physically, but always symbolically, separate the world population into "Us" and "Them" (Yuval-Davis, 2011). Nowadays, people develop transnational identities by travelling between different locations for professional purposes. This is also the case with the Romanian people who migrated in the United Kingdom after January 1, 2014, and after the UK referendum on June 23, 2016.

Moreover, the theme of Romanian people migrating to other countries has launched an intense debate in the media about migration and the national image building problem. In Romania, "migration to other countries is a factor of modernization independent from the state" (Schifirneț, 2012, 46). That is why the freedom to travel after 1989 has lead to a profound revolution in the Romanians' daily thinking and behavior.

After the Revolution of 1989, the image of Romania has become an important theme in the public discourse. It was related to positive and negative evaluations found in the international press, but also on the ways in which Romanians are perceived overseas. Research on the media construction of reality insist on the legitimation of public issues (Dahlgren, 2005; Coleman, Ross, 2010). The focus is on specific themes, "common places", argumentation strategies, but also on rituals and actions used strategically by the social actors in order to "define" the public issue (Beciu, 2011).

For Cefaï, *dramatizing* is essential to legitimate a public problem, because "the social world is a public scene. The actors make use of strategic plans, permanently adapting to game rules comparable to the ones for theatre representations (…). To define roles is to construct dramatic characters (*dramatis personae*)" (2001). As a matter of fact, all the interactions in the public arena have dramatic dimensions. Individuals, groups and institutions compete against each other depending on their social status, in order to impose "definitions", interpretations, and actions. The public arena becomes "fluid", while the debate is constantly reconfigured, depending on the actors that enter the scene (Beciu, 2011).

Gusfield (2001) believes that not any social problem becomes automatically a public one. A public issue is related to competitive interpretations, collective actions and events, decisions or policies. Furthermore, the formation of public issues depends on the socio-historical context, social events, and the political culture. That is why societies do not rely on the same public issues. There are several stages in the formation of a public problem: the audience interest on a certain event, followed by the social actors' interpretations and definitions; the event is imposed on the media agenda by initiating public actions such as governmental decisions, boycotts, or debates (Beciu, 2011).

For instance, the country image is a public issue in Romania which has generated a lot of interpretations and definitions in the public arena. Thus, the country image in the implicit context of migration is not a public issue in other countries, especially in Western Europe. This is due to the fact that the social and political context of post-communist Romania has transformed this event into a public problem.

Research in the area of migration studies concentrate on the role played by mediation in the construction of immigration as a public problem (Mawby & Gisby, 2009; Pijpers, 2006), while others rely on the media framing of intra-EU migration (Balabanova & Balch, 2010, 2016) and on media discourses as sites of symbolic power (Beciu et al, 2017). By analysing communitarian and cosmopolitan frames, Balabanova & Balch (2016) show in their most recent study that communitarian frames dominated discussions of Romanian and Bulgarian migrants. Their study is comparative, analysing UK newspapers in two different periods: 2006 and 2013. Recent research (Cvetkovic & Pantic, 2018) focus on the framing on the European Union borders in live-blogs, discussing about frames such as border management, border as lived spaces, and boders as politically constructed spaces. The results show that borders are framed through complex discursive strategies and processes of negotiation between contested values and attitudes (Cvetkovic & Pantic, 2018, 17). In fact, the continued use of the language of immigration, alongside reference to (Eastern) European migrant or migration - particularly by older EU member states - is revealing of political pressures to limit, dismantle or weaken the institution of free movement (Balch, 2018).

Compared to existing research on migration and the media, this chapter draws on a multidisciplinary approach, combining media studies, public diplomacy, sociology, discourse analysis and semiotics. The focus is on the roles of the journalists in giving their own interpretations to migration as a public problem, in two different communication situations (interactive media campaigns on Romanian migration and news discourses around them) and two different contexts (the freedom of movement to work inside the EU and the British referendum).

Interactive mass-media campaigns as *dispositifs*

It is now time to develop the argument that in today's *network society* (Castells, 2005), the public sphere is a *dynamic* process (Benkler, 2006; Castells, 2008; Dahlgren, 2005; Downey & Fenton, 2003), while the Internet brings new ways of collecting and reporting information into the newsroom. Journalism is becoming more interpretative, while the journalists are actively involving the citizens in the public debate, by initiating media campaigns (Cheregi, 2017).

As Deuze (2004) argues, we experience a *multi-media journalism*, because the presentation of the news story package uses two or more media formats, such as spoken and written word, music, moving and still images, graphic animations, interactive and hypertextual elements. Moreover, a new genre of reporting is emerging, *polymedia events*, understood as events that start in the media and unfold in other media platforms, are transnational in nature, large in scale and audience reach (Madianou & Miller, 2013).

This new journalism involves new writing techniques, adapted to online communications, functions in a network with fragmented audiences and is delivered at great speed (Fenton, 2010: 5-6). Furthermore, the audiences transform into an *active viewer* (Livingstone, 2005), participating in the public debate and interpreting media based on their knowledge and experience.

Related to the changes of the media and the public sphere, this chapter draws on the fact that interactive media campaigns on Romanian migration employ dis courses combining different types of text, visuals and sound, so a multimodal approach is considered. In this particular case, *multimodality* provides the means to describe a practice or representation in all its semiotic complexity (Iedema, 2003).

The interactive media campaigns are all *dispositifs* because they combine text, images, and sound, having a finality defined by the journalists, in order to produce counter-discourses. Firstly, the image, text, and sound are analysed as *semiotic resources*, considering a social semiotic approach (van Leeuwen, 2005; Kress & van Leeuwen, 2006). By appealing to national identity discourses, the journalists construct a social identity for themselves and for their readers. The context (the intensification of discourses on Romanian migration in the British press) is decisive for the communication to occur.

Methodology

In order to analyse how is Romanian migration constructed as a public problem, different communication situations were taken into account: (1) the *controlled* media discourse in specific contexts (campaigns initiated by the media as a response to the anti-immigration discourses from the British tabloid press), and (2) *meta-discourses* around the campaigns. The analysis is based on a mixed design, combining *multimodal* analysis (Iedema, 2003; Kress & van Leeuwen, 2006) with critical discourse analysis (van Dijk, 1993; van Leeuwen, 2008) and *dispositif* analysis (Charaudeau, 2005; Lochard, 2005, 2006; Soulages, 2007).

Foremost, the multimodal approach is necessary in order to investigate the importance of semiotics in image, music and text, considering the ways in which migration is constructed as a public problem through the interactive media campaigns. Moreover, the national and collective identity discourses are understood as *semiotic resources*, from a social semiotic perspective (van Leeuwen, 2005; Kress & van Leeuwen, 2006). The term originated from the work of Halliday (1978, 182), who argued that the grammar of language is not a code, not a set of rules for producing correct sentences, but a "resource for making meanings".

The meanings expressed by the journalists through the campaigns are first and foremost social meanings. The national identity attributes used by the journalists in the media campaigns on Romanian migration are also analysed as *semiotic resources*, considering a social semiotic approach. The semiotic resources are "the actions and artefacts we use to communicate, whether they are produced psychologically [...] or by means of technologies" (van Leeuwen, 2005: 3). By appealing to national identity discourses, the journalist constructs a social identity for the readers. The context (the intensification and mediatization of media discourses on Romanian migration to the UK) is decisive for the communication to occur.

Second of all, critical discourse analysis (CDA) is based on the study of texts as "representation and interaction (strategic or other)" (van Leeuwen, 2008: 4). For Teun van Dijk (1993), the core of the CDA is "a detailed description, explanation and critique of the ways dominant discourses (indirectly) influence socially shared knowledge, attitudes and ideologies, namely through their role in the manufacture of concrete models." As Wodak and Meyer (2009/2014) argue, three concepts figure indispensably in all variants of CDA: critique, power, and ideology. Power is understood as an asymmetric relationship among social actors who assume different social positions or belong to different social groups, while ideology serves as a mean of maintaining unequal power relations through discourse. Moreover, ideology also represents "a general *schemata* that organize the self and the other representations of a group and its members" (van Dijk, 2009/2014: 79).

Therefore, in order to investigate the ways in which media discourses create a polarization between "Us" (Romanian migrants) and "Them" (Britons), the elements of the analysis are: the presence of *constructive strategies* (the linguistic procedures which constitute a national "we-group" and marginalizes the "other-group"); the presence of *argumentation strategies* (justification and questioning of claims of truth and normative rightness); the presence of *nomination strategies* (discursive constructions of social actors (in-groups and out-groups) by membership categorization, verbs and nouns used to denote processes and actions); the presence of *enunciation strategies* (interpolating the readers) and the *attribution of responsibility* (how do the journalists construct the responsibility of the social actors).

Thirdly, the method of *dispositif* analysis (Charaudeau, 2005) will also be applied to see how stereotypes of Romanian people are employed both in the documentary film *Romanians in the UK: Bad timing* (*Adevărul*, March 2014) and the short film *Remainians Respond to Romanians*, made by Britons. The *semio-discursive* analysis (Beciu, 2011; Charaudeau, 2005; Lochard, 2005, 2006; Soulages, 2007) is based on the concept of *communication contract*, defined as a set of conventions that characterize a certain TV broadcast or a media institution. For Charaudeau (2005: 41), the dispositif is

> *a concept that structures the discursive situations, organizing them by considering the participants' position in the interaction process, the nature of their identity and the relations between them depending on certain finality (…). Dispositif also depends on the material conditions that structure the discursive interactions.*

Therefore, the main categories for the *dispositif* analysis are: (1) the thematic orientation of the documentary film, (2) the participants' roles (how are Romanian migrants depicted in the documentary?), (3) the visual framework (conditions to produce a visual discourse, camera angles, types of images, etc.), and (4) the journalist's roles and positioning.

By appealing to national identity discourses, the journalists construct a social identity for themselves and for their readers. The context (the freedom of movement to work in the UK and the Brexit vote) is decisive for the communication to occur.

The data comprises five interactive mass-media campaigns on Romanian migration - Don't Come to Britain! (The Guardian, January 2013), Why Don't You Come Over? (Gândul, January 2013), Let's Change the Story! (Gândul, January 2014), The Truth about Romanians Migrating to the UK (Adevărul, March 2014) and Romanians Adopt Remainians (Gândul, June 2016), along with 100 news articles about the campaigns.

Interactive Media Campaigns on Romanian Migration

At the end of January 2013, the British newspaper *The Guardian* has published an article saying that the Government considers launching a negative ad campaigns in Romania or Bulgaria to persuade potential immigrants to stay away from the UK (Syal, 2013). The headline ("Immigration: Romanian or Bulgarian? You won't like it here") discourages Romanians and Bulgarians to head to Britain, while the lead reinforces this idea: "Please don't come to Britain – it rains and the jobs are scarce and low-paid."

Soon after, *The Guardian* invited its readers to come up with their own ideas for the British Government campaign, aimed at deterring potential immigrants such as Romanians and Bulgarians to come to the UK: "How would you put people off Britain? Send us your posters!" (Walsh, 2013). The journalists have overcome their professional role, engaging the British citizens to involve in the public debate about immigration. The civic role of the journalist is to be seen in helping the citizens to seek solutions for a public problem, independently from political institutions, functioning as "representatives of the society in which they operate as delegates of the culture they share" (Zandberg & Neiger, 2005: 133). The challenge for the readers was addressed by using enunciation strategies:

It may sound like a spoof, but ministers are considering launching a negative advertising campaign in Bulgaria and Romania to try to convince would-be migrants to stay away from the UK.

A report over the weekend quoted one minister saying that such a negative advert would "correct the impression that streets here are paved with gold".

But what would such a poster look like? What aspects of UK life do you think would be most off-putting to those thinking of starting a new life here?

That's where you come in. We feel Guardian readers are well qualified to come up with suggestions of why Britain isn't exactly the best place on earth. Dust off your Photoshop skills and send in your most tongue-in-cheek suggestions as a jpeg or gif

— complete with a caption, if you feel your image needs explaining. We'll publish the best we receive in a gallery. (The Guardian, January 28, 2013)

By inviting the readers to send "tongue-in-cheek" suggestions, the quality newspaper did not take full responsibility for the negative campaign aimed at discouraging migrants to come to Britain. Even though the posters had to be humorous, nationalist discourses still could emerge, as a defense to a possible *invasion*. As Stanca (2013: 75) argues, "humorous adverts are used in online media campaigns to facilitate interpretation of events and to comment on serious political or social issues under the 'safety net' of a non-bona fide mode of communication".

The best posters were published in *The Guardian,* and many humorously deprecated Great Britain, insisting on negative stereotypes such as bad weather, politicians or housing. Overall, the multimodal analysis of the posters shows that irony is a semiotic resource used strategically to create a negative presentation of Great Britain, with the purpose of discouraging Romanians and Bulgarians to come to the UK. Some of the messages sent by the readers were directly addressing Romanian and Bulgarian migrants: "Don't Come to Britain! It's full…of alcopops, asbestos, bad housing, bishops, the British, chavs, Closer magazine, corrupt politicians, cuts, the Daily Mail, dodgy scientists, dogging, drugs with stupid names, drunks, dying bees, dying trees etc. We hate ourselves – we'll probably hate you too", "Great (used to be) Britain. The biggest dump. Go to Australia instead!", "The sky in UK is this color for 8 months a year. Try Miami instead", while implicitly others ridicule the economic bad conditions of the migrants' country of origin: "Come here and clean the loo. Britain is full of horrible jobs we employ foreigners to do. You're welcome!"

As a response to the negative ads putting off migrants, the Romanian newspaper *Gândul* has launched the *Why Don't You Come Over?* campaign in partnership with GMP Advertising agency. With the slogan "We may not like Britain, but you will love Romania. Why don't you come over?" The campaign had two phases: in the first stage, *Gândul* addressed a challenge to their readers, inviting them to come up with ideas, poster designs and slogans to convince Britons to come to Romania, and in the second stage a couch surfing website was created (Why don't you come over, 2016), offering accommodation for Britons who want to travel to Romania.

The slogan is directly addressing to the Britons: "We may not like Britain, but you will love Romania," employing enunciation strategies by interpolating them ("you will love Romania"). Furthermore, the modal auxiliaries "may" and "will" constitute linguistic resources of *modality*, understood as the social semiotic approach to the question of truth (van Leeuwen, 2005: 160). The first part of the slogan "We may not like Britain" relies on low modality, while the second part "but you will love Romania" on medium modality. By employing constructive strategies "we" as a national group, the journalists define their own truth and relate it to the truth of others.

The newspaper *Gândul* proposed its own advertising posters as well, humorously dismissing the British negative portrayal of Romanians. All 12 posters employ stereotypes about Romanians and Britons, using irony support strategies. Moreover, the humorous discourse reveals the journalist's civic role, because "he is less of a mediator, and more of a status actor mobilizing a normative vision about the event's significance" (Beciu, 2011: 217). The journalists from *Gândul* engage the Romanian citizens to involve in the public debate about immigration to Great Britain. They also propose their own definitions and interpretations of the event, coming up with advertising posters aiming to encourage Britons to visit Romania.

After *Gândul* challenged the audience to create its own posters inviting Britons to come to Romania, the response came naturally, because the British negative portrayal of Romanians has threatened citizens' *positive face* (Brown & Levinson: 1978).

For instance, communicative acts such as anti-immigration discourses can threaten citizens' positive face, leading to defensive strategies. In this regard, the advertising posters are to be considered "speech acts" (Searle, 1968), because they have a performative function, so the reader's intention was to give a response to the anti-immigration campaign deterring Romanians and Bulgarians from coming to the UK.

The multimodal analysis of the posters signed by Gândul.info and GMP advertising agency shows that they insist on quotidian life for instance: "Half of our women look like Kate. The other half, like her sister", "Our draft beer is less expensive than your bottled water", transport (for example: "Our Tube was not designed with sardines in mind. Sorry, sardines!", "We have the most beautiful road in the world according to your top motoring show", social aspects (for example "We speak better English than anywhere you've been in France", "Our newspapers are hacking celebrities' privacy, not people's phones"), or political ("Charles bought a house here in 2005. And Harry has never been photographed naked once"). Consequently, the dominant themes are quotidian life and transport.

The auto-irony reveals positive stereotypes about Romania such as beautiful Romanian women, traditional cuisine, language proficiency, affordable living conditions, the convenience of public transport, or Transalpina as the most beautiful road in the world. They reinforce national pride and therefore construct national identity discourses. By using positive stereotypes of Romania and Romanians, the advertising posters appeal to the audience's *positive face* (Brown & Levinson, 1987: 70), treating it as a member of an in-group or a friend. Conversely, irony, "as a transparent dissimulation speech act, changes the sense from positive to negative" (Rovenţa-Frumuşani, 1999: 168), threatening the other's face, by employing negative stereotypes about the British (bad weather, the *tabloidization* of the media, the overcrowded London Tube, the expensive lifestyle, or bad cuisine). Irony is also a ludic act, playing with clichés about British and Romanian people.

An interesting fact is that the advertising posters are designed in the colours of the British flag: blue, red, and white. This leads further to the "banal nationalism" concept (Billig, 1995), because national identity may be reproduced in mediated discourse in ways that go unnoticed. In fact, national identity in the press does not necessarily need to be marked. In today's continual "flagging" or reminding of nationhood, "the metonymic image of banal nationalism is not a flag which is being consciously waved with fervent passion; it is the flag hanging unnoticed on the public building" (Billig, 1995: 8). The flag metaphor suggests the unobserved character of national identity, which is reproduced through communication on various forms like standardized languages or classified words. Continuing this idea, the advertising posters addresses to British people as well, through colours and linguistic deictics such as "you": "We speak better English than anywhere you've been in France".

As a conclusion, the analysis focusing on discursive strategies employed in *Gândul: Why Don't You Come Over?* campaign demonstrates that the journalists from *Gândul* create a polarization between "Us" (Romanian people) and "Them" (British people) by using positive self-presentation strategies and negative other presentation strategies. Moreover, the use of self-deprecating humour reinforces positive stereotypes of Romania and Romanians (beautiful Romanian women, traditional cuisine, intelligent people, affordable economic conditions, convenient public transport). The journalist is no longer a professional journalist, assuming his role as a citizen in the public debate on migration and appealing to the Romanians' national pride. The country image is connected to national identity symbols related to the psychological profile of Romanian people and to the country's modernization in areas such as economy and public transport.

In the light of the anti-immigration media campaign from the British tabloid press, the Romanian newspaper *Gândul* initiated another campaign, in January 2014. Entitled *Let's change the story!*, the focus of the interactive campaign was to contest an article published in the most read British tabloid newspaper, *Daily Mail*. On 31 December 2013, the UK's *Daily Mail* published a story claiming that buses and planes to the UK from Bulgaria and Romania were fully-booked, with the headline: "Sold out! Flights and buses full as

Romanians and Bulgarians head for the UK" (Martin & Stevens, 2013). The article also stated that single plane tickets were selling for up to 3,000 pounds each.

As a response to the article published in Daily Mail the day before the work restrictions to work in the EU, and the UK as well, were to be lifted, the newspaper *Gândul* started an investigation to deconstruct its claims, in collaboration with Jon Danzig (a former investigative journalist at the BBC) and the platform for the EU citizens, New Europeans. The investigative report showed that 60 percent of the information published by Daily Mail was false. For instance, the journalists found out that planes and buses were not full of Romanians and Bulgarians, and tickets were still available at reasonable prices.

Moreover, they spoke directly to the sources quoted in the *Daily Mail* article, in order to check the veracity of the claims. The journalists Alina Matis (Foreign Affairs Editor of *Gândul*) and Jon Danzig did a full deconstruction of all 890 words of the article, making a complaint to the Press Complaints Commission on the grounds of an alleged breach of the Editors Code of Practice.

The campaign involved *Gândul* readers as well, challenging them to sustain the initiative by filling in a form distributed on Facebook. The message addressed to the national group of Romanians (both citizens and readers), appealing to national identity discourses.

The journalists employ *constructive strategies* by using the personal pronoun "we" ("we know", "we invite", "we ask") and the objective pronoun "our" ("This is not our story"). One can notice the presence of a civic journalist, that goes beyond the article investigation and initiates a media campaign involving the Romanian citizens and *Gândul* readers.

The polarization between "Us" (the Romanian press) and "Them" (The British tabloid press) is reinforced by the newspaper's position: "We ask Daily Mail to recognize this false and unfair campaign against Romanians" (Matis, 2014). Power is legitimated in discourse (Wodak & Meyer, 2009/2014: 87), by assuming *Gândul's* position of control. Furthermore, strategies of positive self-presentation (the journalists searching for truth) and negative other presentation (*Daily Mail* as a tabloid newspaper that misinforms its readers) are also used, insisting on the *in-group* good qualities and the *out-group* bad qualities.

Besides this, the campaign orchestrated by *Gândul* and GMP advertising agency proposed a poster saying that "The Daily Mail arrests ten times more Romanians that Scotland Yard". As one can notice, the poster is humorously dismissing *Daily Mail's* quest for truth. Scotland Yard is used as an authoritative argument, while the tabloid *Daily Mail* is above the police law. In line with the advertising posters from *Why Don't You Come Over?* campaign, irony is a discursive strategy used to play with clichés. In this case, negative stereotypes are employed about the most read UK tabloid newspaper, Daily Mail. The focus is on misinformation, revealing the fact that the tabloid presents false news contrasting with information provided by the police.

In fact, the message constitutes a *one-liner* (Norrick, 2000: 171), exhibiting "the two parts necessary to any joke: a build-up, which consists of the orientation and much of the complicating action, and a punchline, which concludes the joke". In the case of the ad poster made by *Gandul.info* and *GMP advertising*, the *punchline* comes in line with the concluding message: "The number of Romanians involved in criminal activities is ten times lower than depicted by tabloids". Numbers are used to deconstruct the *build-up* part, while the antithesis "more" – "lower" reinforces the lack of veracity in the Daily Mail news articles.

Overall, the campaign signals a problem (tabloids such as *Daily Mail* misinform the readers through anti-Romanian discourses), while the solution is provided in the challenge addressed to the *Gândul* readers "Let's Change the Story!". The audience is constructed as participatory by using *interpellation*, so that the reader becomes a subject through ideology, having the power to establish the truth about Romanians in the UK context.

Consequently, the journalists from *Gândul* use irony as a discursive strategy to dismantle Daily Mail's credibility. Positivist arguments are used to suggest the lack of empirical evidence in the news articles about Romanian migrants published in the most read British tabloid newspaper. The journalists employ civic and professional roles, highlighting a problem to the audience and performing an investigation to prove Daily Mail's lack of veracity in the coverage of Romanian migration theme.

An important section of the analysis uses the method of *dispositif* analysis (Charaudeau, 2005) to see how stereotypes of Romanian people are employed both in the documentary film *Romanians in the UK: Bad timing* (*Adevărul*, March 2014) and the short film *Remainians Respond to Romanians* (*Gândul*, June 2016), made by Britons. This method is more suitable for this type of discourse, because the interference of camera angles and different visual frames requires a *semio-discursive* approach (Beciu, 2011), considering the French School (Charaudeau, 2005; Lochard, 2005, 2006; Soulages 2007) perspective.

The main categories for the *dispositif* analysis were: (1) the thematic orientation of the short film, (2) the participants' roles (how are British people depicted in the movie?), (3) the visual framework (conditions to produce a visual discourse, camera angles, types of images, etc.), and (4) the journalist's roles and positioning.

In order to break up the myth of the "Romanian invader" spread in the British media, the Romanian newspaper *Adevărul* has launched a campaign entitled *The Truth about Romanians living in the* UK, in March 2014. The journalists went to London and made a documentary film about the Romanian people that live there, telling stories of successful Romanians that earn millions of pounds, but also stories of Romanians that trick the authorities and stay there illegally.

The *Romanians in the UK: Bad timing* documentary, initiated by the Romanian newspaper *Adevărul,* starts with a frame showing the British-Romanian Police team on action. It continues with visuals showing an old house in the north of London, illegally occupied by Romanians. By selecting one view, scene, or angle, the journalists from *Adevărul* impose their own "definitions" and interpretations about the theme of Romanians migrating to the UK.

Migration is a permanent agenda theme discussed in the documentary and reinforced by the anti-Romanian discourse from the British tabloid press. The secondary themes are pauperization (presenting Romanians illegally living in abandoned houses in the north of London), employment (Romanians working illegally *vs.* Romanians having successful jobs), political implications of migration in Great Britain (interviews with politicians from Labor Party, UKIP, interviews with ambassadors) and the media coverage of migration in the UK (showing headlines from the tabloid press, interviews with British journalists working for the "quality" press).

As for the participant's roles, Romanian migrants are depicted according to their social status: low class Romanians (usually Romanian Roma working illegally in the UK), successful middle and high-class Romanians such as labourers, businessmen, priests, doctors, or lawyers.

Therefore, half of the migrants depicted in the documentary film are Romanian Roma people. Images with Romanians rough sleeping, living illegally, searching for day to day labour in Cricklewood are just a few examples to support unsuccessful stories, reinforcing the anti-Roma discourses found in the Romanian society. For instance, Roma people are generally blamed for anything, "from the insecurity of everyday life (murders, robberies) to the damaging of the country's image abroad" (Boia, 2001).

As for the visual framework, the camera perspective in documentary films is linked to the conditions to produce a visual discourse. Besides this, the frames and sequences are the main *semiotic resources*, constituting the observable actions that have been drawn to the public's attention. According to Gaye Tuchman (1978: 116-121), there are six ways journalists frame subjects on film. The camera may be held at intimate, close personal, far personal, close social, far social or public distance. Each framing convention carries connotations about the social role of the subject or significance of the event.

The most prevalent frame in the documentary film is the *close personal distance* frame, or the medium shot. This is used when filming Romanian Roma people living illegally in the UK, but also when filming Romanian migrants from the middle and high class. The close personal distance frame is preferred in interviews with official sources, such as politicians, journalists, or police officers. In this case, the camera provides a sense of distance, indicating journalistic neutrality. As a discursive effect, the medium shots are used to inform the audience.

The *intimate distance* level is used to show the Romanian migrants' emotions (Figure 1). This frame is rarely used in *Romanians in the UK: Bad timing* documentary, especially when filming Romanians talking about the public issue of migration (such as the barrister Flavia Kenyon or the Orthodox priest Ioan Nazarcu).

Figure 1. Illustrative sample of the intimate distance frame

Thus, the *public distance* frame is used to depict Romanian migrants searching for a job. In this type of shot, the camera is at its furthest distance from the subject, emphasizing the background. The focus of attention is on the social circumstances of migration, favoring migrants as a group rather than individuals. The civic and the evaluator journalists are both present in the documentary film. In fact, the journalist is citizen-oriented, identifying himself with the Romanians by using the objective pronoun "us" and the personal pronoun "we". Therefore, a problem is signalled to the Romanian community, describing the social issue of migration.

As a conclusion, the dominant genre in the documentary film made by *Adevărul* newspaper is the interview, insisting on confession as the main discursive strategy. The main focus is on statutory opinions coming from experts such as British politicians, journalists working for the British "quality" press, police inspectors or sergeants, and intellectual elites (the Romanian barrister and the priest shepherding the Romanian community in Luton). Generally, the statutory opinions converge to the same positioning, criticizing the anti-immigration discourses from the British media and political landscape. Thus, the voices against Romanian migration are also presented in the documentary film, leading to a *deliberative* public sphere (Downey et al., 2012).

At the end of June 2016, the Romanian newspaper Gândul and the advertising agency Webstyler has launched the Romanians Adopt Remainians campaign, just a few days after the EU referendum in the UK. The initiative has encouraged Romanians to reach out to the 16 million Britons who voted to remain in the EU and symbolically adopt them. In this way, the Romanians could help Britons to remain EU citizens by getting a symbolic Romanian identity.

By using *interpellation* to engage Romanian citizens, the journalists also appeal to identity discourses. In this particular case, the focus is on a European common identity: "Fellow Romanians, the good people who voted remain and share European values deserve to be our relatives" (Romanians Adopt Remainians, 2016). Compared to the first two interactive campaigns initiated by the Romanian newspaper *Gândul*, where the journalists used national identity discourses to involve the citizens, in this campaign one can notice the use of European identity.

The British people responded to this campaign through a short movie entitled *Remanians Respond to Romanians*. The movie was published by Gândul.info at the beginning of several articles related to the *Romanians Adopt Remainians* campaign. It starts with a frame showing an advertising poster from the campaign, with the message: "Dear Brits who believe in a united Europe, leave the Brexiters, the quarrelling and the weather behind. Start a brand new life in a loving Romanian family". The following frame shows the title of the film and the British flag waving in the right side. The image is accompanied by the sound of the British anthem, "God Save the Queen".

Labor migration inside the EU is a permanent agenda theme discussed in the short film. The secondary themes are the Brexit vote and Romania's country image. As for the participant's roles, the British people are depicted according to their profession, nationality or hobbies: Reuben works in a chip shop, Linda is from New Zeeland, originally, Charlotte actually met the Queen once, Tom is a crumpet enthusiast, and Valeria is from Italy, originally. Three of the interviewers are British originally, while two of them migrated into the UK.

Considering the visual framework, the most prevalent frame in the documentary film is the *close personal distance* frame (Figure 2), or the medium shot. Usually, this frame is preferred in interviews with official sources. In this case, the camera provides a sense of distance, indicating journalistic neutrality. As a discursive effect, the medium shots are used to inform the audience.

Figure 2. Illustrative sample of the *close personal distance* frame

The *intimate distance* level is used to show people's emotions. In this short movie, the intimate distance shot is used when presenting Tom's emotions regarding the *Romanians Adopt Remainians* campaign: "Thank you for being so gracious and welcoming".

The Romanian journalists are not explicitly present in the film, even though they signal an important problem to the Romanian and British communities. However, the journalists play a civic role, describing the social issue of labor migration through the British citizens' voices.

As a conclusion, the dominant genre in the film made by British citizens for *Gândul* newspaper is the interview, insisting on confession as the main discursive strategy. The main focus is on citizens' opinions regarding the Brexit vote and its implications on labor migration. Overall, they converge to the same positioning, emphasizing the negative effects of Brexit.

Meta-discourses on Romanian migration media campaigns

Now that we have seen how mass-media campaigns on Romanian migration initiated by national newspapers such as *Adevărul* and *Gândul* are constructed, the discussion leads further to the 100 news articles around the campaigns. This will provide an overview of the role of Romanian journalists in shaping the public debate in the context of the British anti-immigration frenzy. Hence, the second part of the analysis insists on *meta-discourses* from a critical discourse analysis (CDA) perspective (Van Dijk, 1993; van Leeuwen, 2008).

A special attention is given to the role of the Romanian journalists in defining migration and, more extensively, the national image as public issues. The question that emerges here is how the roles are constructed in the press articles in relation to discourses on collective and national identity. Furthermore, stereotypes about Romanian people employed in the articles are analysed in depth, in order to see whether they are related to the nation brand issue.

The media discourses around *Gândul – Why Don't You Come Over?* campaign reinforce positive stereotypes of beautiful Romanian women and economic affordability "Mirror: "Romanian women look like Kate and Pipa, and their beer is less expensive than our bottled water". Five out of 27 headlines were focusing on the advertising posters, reinforcing discourses employed in the campaign.

Secondly, the news discourses around *Gândul – Let's Change the Story!* campaign insists on the choice of a designator such as "Daily Fail" instead of Daily Mail. A total of four out of 17 news headlines contain the expression "Daily Fail", revealing a strong position from *Gândul* newspaper. The catchphrase constitutes a semiotic resource as well, drawing observable actions (the inaccurate story about Romanian and Bulgarian migrants published by *Daily Mail*) into the domain of social communication. The journalists also use expressions such as "Daily Mail, the speaking trumpet of the anti-Romanian and anti-Bulgarian media campaign", "hordes of Romanians, and Bulgarians", "the Romanian invasion" and "Romanian phobia".

The polarization between "Us" (the Romanian press) and "Them" (the British tabloid press) is strengthened by the negative other presentation (*Daily Mail* as a speaking trumpet for the anti-Romanian campaign).

Overall, the expert and civic roles are prevalent in the news discourse around *Let's Change the Story!* campaign. The media discourses employ strategies of involvement to transform readers into citizens and *active viewers* (Livingstone 2005). "Let's rewrite the story of Romanians in Europe and put public pressure for reporting the truth in newspapers such as Daily Mail" (Matiş 2014).

Thirdly, in the press articles about *Adevărul - The Truth about Romanians migrating to the UK* campaign, military discourse is dominant: "the British crusade against Romanians", "Romanian migrants became ammunition in the British offensive against immigrants".

The stylistic choices made by journalists from *Adevărul* are based on catchphrases such as "invader nation", "racism", "prejudice", "hysteria regarding the "thousands" of Romanians that will "invade" Great Britain, "inventing news", "aggressive denigration campaign", "Romanian migrants became ammunition in the British offensive against immigrants", "scapegoats" ,"the Romanian invader myth", "the lethal tango between press and politics", and "the British crusade against Romanians". These linguistic structures are semiotic resources, suggesting the ideology of the journalists, based on the principles that the press should be objective and truthful, and not inventive and deceiving.

As for the *Romanians Adopt Remainians* campaign, here the focus of the news articles was on negative stereotypes about Britons, interpellation and European identity. *Remainians* is used as a semiotic resource, while one can notice the appeal to a European identity: "a symbolic exercise of solidarity, which is one of the fundamental principles of European construction" (Dinu, 2016).

Conclusion

The multi-modal analysis provided in this chapter proves that Romanian journalists have overcome their role as professionals in order to assume a civic role by involving the citizens in the public debate on migration, and, more extensively, on the country image problem.

Furthermore, the journalists from Gândul and Adevărul initiate interactive mass-media campaigns such as Why Don't You Come Over?, Let's Change the Story!, The truth about Romanians migrating to the UK, or Romanians Adopt Remainians in order to respond to media campaigns aim to discourage Romanians and Bulgarians to come to the UK (Don't Come to Britain!, The Guardian, January 2013). By combining heterogeneous elements such as text, visuals, and sound, the campaigns are all dispositifs, having a finality defined by the journalists, which is their aim to produce counter-discourses. Although dispositifs mix several types of discourses, the roles of the journalists share some similarities in the three interactive campaigns. In this regard, there are three roles preferred: the expert (the professional journalist), the deliberative (mediating between different perspectives on the migration issue) and the civic journalist (challenging the audience to actively participate in the campaigns). In all campaigns, the journalists create a polarization between "Us" (Romanian people) and "Them" (British people) by using positive self-presentation strategies and negative other presentation strategies.

The analysis was focused around mass-media campaigns as journalistic products. The five interactive media campaigns are all *dispositifs*, employing positive stereotypes about Romania and Romanians, such as beautiful Romanian women, people's intelligence, affordable economic conditions, convenient public transport, professionalism, and altruism. All campaigns challenged the audience to participate in the debate on migration, by *interpellating* its readers. Taking into account the discursive strategies, the *Why Don't You Come Over?* and *Let's Change the Story!* campaigns were based on self-deprecating humor, and the messages constituted *one-liners* (Norrick, 2000). This response came naturally, once the British negative portrayal of Romanians has threatened citizens' *positive face* (Brown & Levinson, 1978). As for the *Romanians Adopt Remainians* campaign irony was employed as a discursive strategy to emphasize negative stereotypes about British people.

Besides this, the dominant genre in the documentary film *Romanians in the UK: Bad timing* (*Adevărul*, March 2014), and in the short film made *Remainians Respond to Romanians* (*Gândul*, June 2016) is the interview, insisting on confession as the main discursive strategy. In the *Remainians Respond to Romanians* short movie, the main focus is on citizens' opinions regarding the Brexit vote and its implications on labor migration. Overall, they converge to the same positioning, emphasizing the negative effects of Brexit. Even though the Romanian journalists are not explicitly present in the film, they play a civic role, describing the social issue of labor migration through the British citizens' voices.

The second part of the analysis revolved around the news discourse about the campaigns. The results of the critical discourse analysis show that media discourses around *Why Don't You Come Over?* campaign reinforce positive stereotypes about Romanian women and economic affordability. In *Let's Change the story!* campaign, four out of 17 news headlines use *Daily Fail* as a semiotic resource. In the news articles around *The truth about Romanians migrating to the UK* campaign, one can notice the use of a military discourse "the British crusade against Romanians". As for *Romanians adopt Remainians*, the media discourses focused around the use of *Remainians* as a semiotic resource. Compared to the previous campaigns, where the focus was on national identity, here the focus was on a European identity.

One of the main questions addressed in this chapter is how the Romanian journalists define Romania's country image in the interactive media campaigns on migration. The investigation reveals that the country image is addressed in relation to the psychological profile of Romanian people, to the country's modernization in areas such as economy and public transport, to Europeanization (Romania after the EU accession), history (the transition period), and to neoliberal discourses (the Dracula myth).

In the context of the increasing importance of mediated communication, observing the dynamics and interactions between various communicative actors (the press and the audience) is relevant. Moreover, future studies should consider the extent to which the press transforms the public into *active viewers* (Livingstone, 2005) through the frames they employ. A special attention should be given to audience's reactions to situations when public problems are at stake.

Acknowledgement

This work was supported by a grant of the Romanian Ministry of Research and Innovation, CNCS – UEFISCDI, project number PN-III-P1-1.1-BSH-2-2016-0005, within PNCDI III, during the "Spiru Haret Fellowship", 2017-2018.

References

Balabanova, E., & Balch, A. (2010). Sending and Receiving: the Ethical Framing of intra-EU migration in the European press. *European Journal of Communication*, (25), 382–397.

Balch, A., & Balabanova, E. (2016). Ethics, Politics and Migration: Public Debates on the Free Movement of Romanian and Bulgarians in the UK, 2006-2013. *Politics, 36*(1), 19-35.

Balch, A. (2018). The Politics of Intra-European Movement. In *Between Mobility and Migration The Multi-Level Governance of Intra-European Movement* (IMISCOE Research Series). Springer.

Beciu, C. (2012). Diaspora și experiența transnațională, practici de mediatizare în presa românească [Diaspora and the transnational experience, mediating practices in the Romanian press]. *Romanian Journal of Sociology*, (1-2), 49–66.

Beciu, C. (2013). Discursive Reprensentations of Migrants in Political Talk-Shows in Romania. *Romanian Journal of Sociology*, (1-2), 41–62.

Beciu, C., Mădroane, I. D., Ciocea, M., & Cârlan, A. (2017). Media engagement in the transnational social field: discourses and repositionings on migration in the Romanian public sphere. *Critical Discourse Studies*, 1–17. https://doi.org/10.1080/17405904.2017.1284682.

Benkler, Y. (2006). *The Wealth of Networks: How Social Production Transforms Markets and Freedom*. New Haven, CT: Yale University Press.

Billig, M. (2002). *Banal Nationalism*. London: Sage Publications.

Boswell, C., & Geddes, A. (2009). *Migration and Mobility in the European Union*. Red Globe Press.

Brown, P., & Levinson, S. (1987). *Politeness: some universals in language usage*. Cambridge: Cambridge University Press.

Brunnbauer, U. (2009). *Transnational Societies, Transterritorial Politics. Migrations in the (post-) Yugoslav Region, 19th-21st Century.* Oldenbourg: Oldenbourg Verlag.

Castells, M. (2008). The New Public Sphere: Global Civil Society, Communication Networks and Global Governance. *The Annals of the American Academy of Political and Social Science, 616*(1), 78 – 93.

Castells, M., & Cardoso, G. (2005). *The Network Society. From Knowledge to Policy.* Washington, DC: Johns Hopkins Center for Transatlantic Relations.

Castles, S., & Miller, M. J. (2003). *The Age of Migration.* New York: Guilford Press.

Cefaï, D. (2001). Les cadres de l'action collective. Définitions et problemes. In D. Cefaï & D. Trom, *Mobilisations dans les arènes publiques.* Paris: Ehess.

Charaudeau, P. (2005). *Le discours politique – Les masques du puvoir.* Paris: Vuibert.

Cheregi, B.-F. (2017). "Let's Change the Story!": Nation Branding and Interactive Media Campaigns on Romanian Migration. In *Exploring Communication through Qualitative Research* (pp. 20–40). UK: Cambridge Scholars Publishing.

Cheregi, B.-F. (2018a). *Nation Branding in Post-Communist Romania. A semiotic approach.* Bucharest: comunicare.ro.

Cheregi, B.-F. (2018b). The Media Framing of Migration in Sending and Receiving countries: The Case of Romanians Migrating to the UK. In *Gendering Nationalism. Intersections of Nation, Gender and Sexuality.* UK: Palgrave Macmillan.

Ciocea, M., & Cârlan, A. (2012). Debating Migration as a Public Problem: Diasporic Stances in Media Discourse. *Romanian Journal of Communication and Public Relations,* (27), 181–201.

Couldry, N. (2008). Mediatization or mediation? Alternative understandings of the emergent space of digital storytelling. *New Media & Society, 10*(3), 373–391.

Couldry, N., & Hepp, A. (2013). Conceptualizing Mediatization: Contexts, Traditions, Arguments, *23*(3), 191–202.

Cvetkovic, I., & Pantic, M. (2018). Multimodal Discursivity: Framing European Union Borders in Live-Blogs. *Journal of Communication Inquiry,* 1–22. https://doi.org/10.1177/0196859918786273.

Dahlgren, P. (2005). The Internet, Public Spheres, and Political Communication: Dispersion and Deliberation. *Political Communication,* (22), 147–162.

Deuze, M. (2004). Journalism studies beyond media: On ideology and identity. *Ecquid Novi: African Journalism Studies, 25*(2), 275–293.

Downey, J., & Fenton, N. (2003). New Media, Counter Publicity and the Public Sphere. *New Media Society, 5*(2), 185–202.

Fenton, N. (2010). *New Media, Old News. Journalism & Democracy in the Digital Age.* London: Sage Publications.

Halliday, M. (1978). *Language as Social Semiotic.* London: Edward Arnold.

Hobolt, S. B. (2016). The Brexit vote: a divided nation, a divided continent. *Journal of European Public Policy, 23*(9), 1259–1277. https://doi.org/10.1080/13501763. 2016.1225785.

Iedema, R. (2003). Multimodality, resemiotization: extending the analysis of discourse as multi-semiotic practice. *Visual Communication, 2*(1), 29–57.

Kress, G., & Van Leeuwen, T. (2006). *Reading Images: the Grammar of Visual Design.* London: Routledge.

Livingstone, S. (2005). *Audiences and Publics: When Cultural Engagement matters for the Public Sphere.* Bristol: Intellect Books.

Livingstone, S. (2009). On the mediation of everything. *Journal of Communication, 59*(1), 1–18.

Lochard, G. (2005). *L'Information Televisée: Mutations Professionnelles Et Enjeux Citoyens.* Paris: Vuibert.

Lochard, G. (2006). *Les débats publics dans les télévisions européens.* Paris: L'Harmattan.

Lundby, K. (2014). *Mediatization of Communication*. Mouton de Gruyter.

Madianou, M. (2013). Humanitarian campaigns in social media: Network architectures and polymedia events. *Journalism Studies, 14*(2), 249–266.

Madianou, M., & Miller, D. (2013). Polymedia: Towards a new theory of digital media in interpersonal
communication. *International Journal of Cultural Studies, 16*(2), 169–187.

Martin, A., & Stevens, J. (2013). Sold out! Flights and buses full as Romanians and Bulgarians head for the UK. Retrieved from http://www.dailymail.co.uk/news/article-2531440/Sold-Flights-buses-Romanians-Bulgarians-head-UK.html

Matiş, A. (2014). Susţine campania Gândul - Let's change the story! Efectul anchetei prin care demonstram că 60 la sută dintr-un articol Daily Mail e fals: un membru al Guvernului britanic recunoaşte minciunile din retorica anti-români. Retrieved from http://www.gandul.info/international/sustine-campania-gandul-let-s-change-the-story-efectul-anchetei-demonstram-60-suta-dintr-articol-daily-mail-e-fals-membru-guvernului-britanic-recunoaste-minciunile-retorica-anti-romani-12015456

Mawby, R. C., & Gisby, W. (2009). Crime, Media and Moral Panic in an Expanding European Union. *The Howard Journal of Criminal Justice, 48*(1), 37–51.

Norrick, N. R. (2000). *Conversational Narrative: Storytelling in Everyday Talk*. Amsterdam: John Benjamins Publishing Company.

Pijpers, R. (2006). "Help! The Poles are Coming" Narrating a Contemporary Moral Panic. *Geografiska Annaler: Series B, Human Geography, 88*(1), 91–103.

Rajeev, S. (2013, January 27). Immigration: Romanian or Bulgarian? You won't like it here. Retrieved from https://www.theguardian.com/uk/2013/jan/27/uk-immigration-romania-bulgaria-ministers.

Redden, J., & Witschge, T. (2010). A new news order. Online news content examined. In N. Roselle,

L. (2003). Local Coverage of the 2000 Election in North Carolina: Does Civic Journalism Make a Difference? *American Behavioral Scientist, 46*(5), 600–615.

Rovenţa-Frumuşani, D. (1999). *Semiotică, societate, cultură [Semiotics, Society, Culture]*. Bucharest: European Institute.

Schifirneţ, C. (2012). Tendential Modernity. *Social Science Information, 51*(1), 22–51.

Silverstone, R. (2007). *Media and Morality: On the Rise of the Mediapolis*. Cambridge: Polity.

Soulages, J.-C. (2007). *Les rhétoriques télévisuelles. Les images-mondes du petit écran*. Paris: De Boeck Supérieur.

Stanca, M. (2013). Interpreting Humorous Adverts in Online Media. *Philology and Cultural Studies, 6*(2), 73–79.

Tuchman, G. (1978). *Making News. A Study in the Construction of Reality*. New York: The Free Press.

van Dijck, J., & Poell, T. (2014). Making Public Television Social? Public Service Broadcasting and the Challenges of Social Media. *Television & New Media, 16*(2), 148–164.

Van Leeuwen, T. (2005). *Introducing Social Semiotics*. London: Routledge.

Walsh, J. (2013, January 28). How would you put people off Britain? Send us your posters. Retrieved from https://www.theguardian.com/uk/2013/jan/28/migrants-britain-rubbish-posters

Wodak, R., De Cillia, R., & Reisigl, M. (1999). The discursive construction of national identities. *Discourse and Society, 10*(2), 149 – 173.

Yuval-Davis, N. (2011). *The Politics of Belonging: Intersectional Contestations*. London: Sage Publications.

Zandberg, E., & Neiger, M. (2005). Between the nation and the profession: journalists as members of contradicting communities. *Media, Culture & Society, 27*(1), 131–141. https://doi.org/10.1177/0163443705049073

CHAPTER 6

SOCIAL MEDIA AND ICT USE BY REFUGEES, IMMIGRANTS AND NGOS: A LITERATURE OVERVIEW

Bilgen Türkay

Introduction

Use of Information and Communication Technologies has been getting both more advanced and widespread in last few decades. The universal definition of the term is generally accepted to mean all devices, networking components, applications and systems that combined allow people and organizations to interact in the digital world. Generally, it includes antiquate technologies such as television broadcast, radio and landline telephones, as well as smartphones, internet enabled computers and cutting-edge machines such as artificial intelligence and robotics.[1] In this paper, ICT refers to all digital devices including computers and smartphones.

A non-governmental organization (NGO) is a non-profit, voluntary citizens' group which is organized on a local, national or international level. Task – oriented and driven by people with a common interest, NGOs perform a variety of services and humanitarian functions.[2] In this paper, NGO states all non-governmental actors who help refugees and immigrants.

Emerging telecommunication technologies such as widespread internet access and smartphones can alter experiences of time and space for refugees, and change the power relationships (e.g. Hinchliffe, 1996; Pfaff, 2010). Some argue that smartphones are as essentials for migrants as food and shelter in the 21st century (Brunwasser, 2015). Despite the potential power and influence of ICT and social media, there has been little consideration of the particular importance technology hold for refugees and immigrants: individuals who are affected by problems of migration and marginalization. Recent studies have covered a range of technologies and context including how online mapping technologies can be used to engage refugees in camp

---

[1] https://searchcio.techtarget.com/definition/ICT-information-and-communications-technology-or-technologies

[2] http://www.ngo.org/ngoinfo/define.html

activities together with international organizations; how mobile phones could be used to enable refugees to migrate and resolve uncertainties of everyday life; and how computer clubs could be established to foster learning, social networks and integration with local communities (e.g., Xu & Maintland, 2016). ICT has changed living practices including how people learn, work or communicate and has made them easier. These technologies can possibly have critical role in NGOs efforts when helping strategies to refugees and immigrants during different stages of their journey.

Various media-related needs were pronounced in wartime compared to peacetime because of higher uncertainty and increasing media coverage (Dotan & Cohen, 1976). These needs can be analyzed in four main categories of Uses and Gratification needs (Dolan, Conduit, Fahy & Goodman, 2016): cognitive (to know what is happening and to understand the possible outcomes of events), affective (to be entertained and to maintain a high morale); social-integrative (to trust the nation's leaders and be proud in the country); and escapist (to "kill time" and escape loneliness). In addition to these, a fifth category called survivalist, was added by Kozman and Melki (2017). On this latter point, Wall, Otis Campbell and Janbek (2015)'s study of Syrian refugees found that refugees view mobile phones within a broader political context. They found that the refugees think mobile phones played a crucial role in the revolution and thanks to mobile phones, the world found out what was happening in Syria.

In this paper, we provide an overview of the findings from recent studies on refugees, immigrants' and NGOs' use of ICT and social media to answer the following questions:

- Why do refugees and immigrant use social media and ICT?

- What are the barriers of using social media and ICT by refugees and immigrants?

- How do NGOs' use social media and ICT to help refugees and immigrants?

- What are the barriers of using and social media and ICT by NGOs'?

In addition to providing answers to these questions with the purpose of providing a snapshot on refugees' and migrants' use of ICT and social media, this work aims to inform NGOs in the ways they can most effectively reach these groups of people using emerging technologies.

In addition to providing answers to these questions with the purpose of providing a snapshot on refugees' and migrants' use of ICT and social media, this work aims to inform NGOs in the ways they can most effectively reach these groups of people using emerging technologies.

Findings

In this section, we present our findings to the four research questions.

Why Refugees And Immigrant Use Ict And Social Media?

In this study, five main reasons are found for ICT and social media use by refugees and immigrants: communication, information seeking, content creation and sharing, entertainment and escaping, as well as for surviving. Below are the details on these reasons:

Communication

Communication is one of the most important and prevalent reasons to use ICT and social media. Mobile phones are salient devices of communication during refugees' journey from their native country to the host countries. During this journey and afterwards, mobile phones serve multiple purposes to help maintain "transnational ties" (Vertovec, 2009: 61). In recent years, thanks to the advancements in network capabilities, Internet has become more tool for communication for refugees and immigrants. According to AFAD[3] reports in 2017,[4] while %75.80 of Syrian refugees in Turkey prefer internet to communicate with their families live in Syria, %21.10 of Syrian refugees in Turkey prefer to communicate through their mobile phones.

For those who did not have the Internet access on their phones, cybercafés were important hubs to access the Internet as well as to socialise with others who are in the same journey with them. In an ethnographic study, Charmarkeh (2013) explored refugees' uses of social media during their migratory path, from Somalia to France, and settlement in three French cities. The majority of participants stated that during their entire journey they would use cybercafés in order to gain access to the Internet and telephone. During their journey, refugees use the Internet was essentially for the purpose of communicating and that they use the phone for emergency situations. Once arrived in France, Somalis extend their usage of media to include traditional forms, particularly television.

Similar results were found by Cassar, Gauci, & Bacchi (2016) who conducted a survey study with 169 migrants from 44 countries in Malta on their use of social media. Respondents were categorized in three groups: EU

---

[3] T.C. Başbakanlık Afet ve Acil Durum Yönetimi Başkanlığı
[4] Türkiye'deki Suriyeliler Demografik Görünümü, Yaşam Koşulları ve Gelecek Beklentilerine yönelik Saha Araştırması. https://www.afad.gov.tr/upload/Node/25337/xfiles/17a-Turkiye_deki_Suriyelilerin_Demografik_Gorunumu_Yasam_Kosullari_ve_Gelecek_Beklentilerine_Yonelik_Saha_Arastirmasi_2017.pdf

citizens, asylum seekers, and other TCNs[5] in order to explore whether information and communication needs as well as internet access differ between these migrant groups. They found that refugee's access social media to transmit and receive information to and from their families by sending and receiving personal messages primarily to friends, family members, and acquaintances (e.g., chatting and sharing photos). Facebook was the most commonly used social media site which helped immigrants to keep in contact with extant friends and family, and to create new connections and relationships with those in their new locations (Panagakos & Horst, 2006; Gillespie et al., 2016). Similar purposes of usage were detected among immigrant populations and asylum seekers as well.

In one study with tertiary students from five migrant or ethnic minority groupings in Auckland, Marlowe, Bartley and Collins (2017) investigated the ways in which social media and digital interactions influence students' sense of belongingness that create *'situatedness'* for participants. While participants usually used social media to maintain relationships across geographically dispersed family networks, their local relationships were also intensified through using various social media platforms which supplemented face-to-face contact. As migrants, the participants had experiences of maintaining meaningful transnational relationships, and the range of connective media platforms enabled forms of connectedness that would otherwise be impossible. Engagement with social media has also brought some into new networks of belonging, with contacts that they might never engage in face-to-face interchanges.

In their study of ICT usage in detention camps for asylum seekers in Australian island, Coddington and Mountz (2014) found that migrants in both island and mainland sites of detention use technology and social media to combat isolation by forging networks that transcend these vast distances. They found that asylum seekers use mobile phone calls, text messaging, websites, Skype, Facebook, and Twitter to communicate with people and counter the remoteness and isolation of detention facilities, and to maintain their relationships built in detention. They also use technology to contact outside advocates about protest actions, health emergencies, and other urgent activities. Similar results were found in studies done with Syrian refugees in Lebanon (Yap & Leffler, 2017) and Jordan (Xu, & Maitland, 2016). Particularly, Syrian youth preferred to use WhatsApp and Facebook to communicate.

In summary, refugees need to communicate during their journey as well as after they arrive to their destination country to keep contact with their families, and to transmit what they experienced and learned, and receive

---

[5] TCN: Third Country Nationals

information about the current situation back home. The digital environment makes relationships that were constrained by geographical distance more common and more meaningful (Marlowe et al., 2017).

Information seeking: Looking back and preparing for the forth

Refugees and immigrants use both traditional (e.g., television) and social media for surveillance, to follow news about their country in conflict, to collect information on specific topics such to look for migration-related information or product service reviews that would be important in their destination countries (Cassar, Gauci, & Bacchi, 2016; Leffler & Yap, 2017). Wall, Otis Campbell and Janbek (2015) examined how Syrian refugees living in Jordan were using cell phones to cope with what they called information precarity, a term referring to the condition of instability that refugees experience in accessing news and personal information, potentially leaving them vulnerable to misinformation, stereotyping, and rumours that can affect their economic and social capital. Based on focus groups conducted in a Jordanian refugee camp, they found refugees experienced information precarity in five forms: (1) technological and social access to information; (2) the prevalence of irrelevant, sometimes dangerous information; (3) lack of their own image control; (4) surveillance by the state; and (5) disrupted social support. Refugees identified news as one of the key pieces of content that they both sought and disseminated themselves. They used phones as their tool for the Internet access and perceive phones a powerful tools for their role in the revolution.

Hannides, Bailey and Kaoukji (2016) conducted in-depth interviews with refugees in Greece and Germany. The main reason for refugees to use ICT was to get timely and reliable information on how to get to their next destination safely, quickly and without being detained. On the other hand, Cassar et al. (2016) found that only slightly more than one-third of respondents report to seek information on the country of destination on the social media. However, the authors did not find why such low number of participants did so: do refugees view information in social media as unreliable or impersonal? Or, whether it is because there is not enough of it for social media platforms to be considered to be sources of such information, or because this is simply not a priority in social media use for migrants. A large majority asked to receive more information on migrant rights and law regulations via their community's social media channels than they usually do.

On the other hand, in their case study, Kozman and Melki (2017) surveyed 1820 displaced Syrian nationals in four countries (Lebanon - 28%, Jordan -24%, Syria-40%, and Turkey-8%) to explore the news consumption habits of war refugees. They found that Syrian individuals' need for information was among the most frequent uses of all types of media, both new and traditional, and social media and news websites were ranked as highly important for daily news about Syria. Refugees and immigrants consider host media as windows of reality of the host culture, their ethnic media use helps link them and provides them with a connection to their ethnic group (Jeffres & Hur, 1981).

AFAD's report in 2017[6] shows that %61.60 of Syrian refugees who lives in the refugee camps in Turkey get information about Syria from internet. While %30 of refugees use television and radio, %5.10 of refugees get information from their friends. On the other hand, %25.60 of Syrian refugees who live outside of the refugee camps use internet for getting information about Syria. While %65.80 get news from television or radio, %6.40 of refugees get them from their friends.

In summary, "information is a basic need in humanitarian response" (2013 UN OCHA). Timely access to information empowers individuals, families, and communities to better serve their own interests, whether it is about the country they left behind or the new lands ahead. As the proliferation of the Internet and mobile phones only increases, it is almost certain that future humanitarian emergencies will have to contend with providing communications to both the responder and crisis-affected populations in almost every emergency. The findings from prior studies implies that organizations aim to connect with refugees and migrants via social media should both establish a personal connection with these groups, and may choose influential people who are trusted by refugees and migrant.

Information seeking: Looking back and preparing for the forth

Refugees and immigrants use both traditional (e.g., television) and social media for surveillance, to follow news about their country in conflict, to collect information on specific topics such to look for migration-related information or product service reviews that would be important in their destination countries (Cassar, Gauci, & Bacchi, 2016; Leffler & Yap, 2017). Wall, Otis Campbell and Janbek (2015) examined how Syrian refugees living in Jordan were using cell phones to cope with what they called information precarity, a term referring to the condition of instability that refugees experience in accessing news and personal information, potentially leaving them vulnerable to misinformation, stereotyping, and rumours that can affect their economic and social capital. Based on focus groups conducted in a Jordanian refugee camp, they found refugees experienced information

---

[6] Türkiye'deki Suriyeliler Demografik Görünümü, Yaşam Koşulları ve Gelecek Beklentilerine yönelik Saha Araştırması. https://www.afad.gov.tr/upload/Node/25337/xfiles/17a-Turkiye_deki_Suriyelilerin_ Demografik_Gorunumu_Yasam_Kosullari_ve_Gelecek_Beklentilerine_Yonelik_Saha_Arastirmasi_201 7.pdf

precarity in five forms: (1) technological and social access to information; (2) the prevalence of irrelevant, sometimes dangerous information; (3) lack of their own image control; (4) surveillance by the state; and (5) disrupted social support. Refugees identified news as one of the key pieces of content that they both sought and disseminated themselves. They used phones as their tool for the Internet access and perceive phones a powerful tools for their role in the revolution.

Hannides, Bailey and Kaoukji (2016) conducted in-depth interviews with refugees in Greece and Germany. The main reason for refugees to use ICT was to get timely and reliable information on how to get to their next destination safely, quickly and without being detained. On the other hand, Cassar et al. (2016) found that only slightly more than one-third of respondents report to seek information on the country of destination on the social media. However, the authors did not find why such low number of participants did so: do refugees view information in social media as unreliable or impersonal? Or, whether it is because there is not enough of it for social media platforms to be considered to be sources of such information, or because this is simply not a priority in social media use for migrants. A large majority asked to receive more information on migrant rights and law regulations via their community's social media channels than they usually do.

On the other hand, in their case study, Kozman and Melki (2017) surveyed 1820 displaced Syrian nationals in four countries (Lebanon - 28%, Jordan -24%, Syria-40%, and Turkey-8%) to explore the news consumption habits of war refugees. They found that Syrian individuals' need for information was among the most frequent uses of all types of media, both new and traditional, and social media and news websites were ranked as highly important for daily news about Syria. Refugees and immigrants consider host media as windows of reality of the host culture, their ethnic media use helps link them and provides them with a connection to their ethnic group (Jeffres & Hur, 1981).

AFAD's report in 2017[7] shows that %61.60 of Syrian refugees who lives in the refugee camps in Turkey get information about Syria from internet. While %30 of refugees use television and radio, %5.10 of refugees get information from their friends. On the other hand, %25.60 of Syrian refugees who live outside of the refugee camps use internet for getting information

---

[7] NetHope is an information technology collaboration of 37 leading international nongovernmental organizations (NGOs) representing more than $30 billion (U.S.) of humanitarian development, emergency response, and conservation programs serving millions of beneficiaries in more than 180 countries. Through member collaboration and by facilitating public-private partnerships with major technology companies, foundations, and individuals, NetHope helps members use their technology investments to better serve people in the most remote areas of the world. Currently NetHope membership consists of international NGOs including: CARE, Catholic Relief Services, International Federation of Red Cross and Red Crescent Societies, Mercy Corps, Oxfam, Save the Children, and World Vision, among others.

about Syria. While %65.80 get news from television or radio, %6.40 of refugees get them from their friends.

In summary, "information is a basic need in humanitarian response" (2013 UN OCHA). Timely access to information empowers individuals, families, and communities to better serve their own interests, whether it is about the country they left behind or the new lands ahead. As the proliferation of the Internet and mobile phones only increases, it is almost certain that future humanitarian emergencies will have to contend with providing communications to both the responder and crisis-affected populations in almost every emergency. The findings from prior studies implies that organizations aim to connect with refugees and migrants via social media should both establish a personal connection with these groups, and may choose influential people who are trusted by refugees and migrant.

Contents sharing and creation

Refugees and migrants use media for the purposes of creating and sharing or helping others to create and share information as well as sharing creative work, targeting large audiences beyond personal acquaintances. Examples include recording videos for YouTube or owning/ administering a Facebook page for their communities (Cassar, Gauci, & Bacchi, 2016). Alhayek (2016) suggest that the access to ICT tools such as mobile phones and the Internet allowed people to document the Syrian regime's violations and share them with the world, which was not possible in the first activist movement in the early 1980s. During the peaceful phase of the Syrian uprising, ICTs helped activists to film and document the actions of the Syrian regime and share these with the rest of the world through social media, which also helped in igniting new protests. However, the same ICTs became a weapon in the hands of the Syrian regime as a way to monitor, attack, and trace activists.

For asylum seekers, Twitter was a key resource for spreading information. For example, residents and people in detention on Nauru with access to cell phones tweet under the hashtag #Nauru about asylum seeker arrivals and departures, health issues, and conditions of detention (e.g., Deidenang, 2013). Asylum seekers also use email, Facebook, and text messages to inform advocates outside detention about new arrivals, including names, countries of origin, and boat numbers in their detention facility as well as others detained in other locations (Coddington and Mountz, 2014).

It is worth noting that despite the extensive media coverage of migrant crisis since the Syrian war started, there has been very little coverage of migrants' and refugees' own personal stories and images (Gillespie et al., 2016). Perhaps an exemption was selfies migrants took of themselves. According to Chouliaraki (2017), selfies serve many purposes in refugees' journey. Among those are self-representation as celebration (i.e., showing smiling migrants at the entry points into Europe from the Turkey coast, emphasizing their existence or location); self-representation as recognition (i.e., selfies that migrants have taken with celebrities, such as Angela Merkel and Pope Francis, standing in solidarity with them in detention camps around Europe); and self-representation as erasure (i.e., celebrities impersonating migrants to protest against Europe's response to the migration crisis). The author defines these different ways of representation as "symbolic bordering" which defines the systematic removal of migrants' authentic representations from meaningful participation in Western public dialogue.

Mobile phones also provide critical updates to asylum seekers' journeys. For example, pictures from a mobile phone helped to publicize the sinking of a boat with asylum seekers on board in Indonesian waters in 2013 (Jones & Wires, 2013). Facebook sites devoted to advocacy and the status of asylum seekers detained in various places have become important resources for asylum seekers in detention and advocates to connect. Advocates publish information about protests, educational campaigns, and other activities to demonstrate their support for refugees; and asylum seekers in turn—usually anonymously—publish information about recent arrivals, protest actions from within detention centres, and health issues. For example, a posting from the "Asylum Seekers on Nauru" Facebook site described poor conditions on the island, explicitly addressing alerting advocates and media. Asylum seekers publish pictures, artwork, news articles, and describe the conditions of detention on these sites, engaging directly with members of the media, nongovernmental organizations, and advocacy groups.

However, content creation and sharing activities are less common among refugees and those who are involved in these activities are more likely to hold at least a post-secondary education. Cassar et al. (2016) note that volunteer organisations should work towards empowering migrants online and assist them in developing and creating content that would be useful to them and to their friends and networks. This would also help building capacity among refugee communities and may improve their digital literacies.

Entertainment and escaping

Entertainment is one of the topmost reasons people use both traditional and social media in their daily lives. While it may be less important during wars, using media for entertainment is still a need for refugees. Refugees use newspapers and social media to seek entertainment (Cassar, Gauci, & Bacchi, 2016) in order to maintain high morale and, and escape the reality of war and surviving. Marlowe et al. (2017) notes that digital technologies actively contribute to the scope and quality of everyday life for immigrants, playing a part in individuals' 'sense of belonging', generating 'happiness' and feelings of interconnection. ICT and social media use is very important for refugees' psychological wellbeing. Hannides et al. (2016)'s found that refugees who stay in regular contact with other refugees and who have wide communication networks of family members and friends via mobile networks and social networking sites such as Facebook and WhatsApp were likely to be more resilient than those who were less connected.

While the need to maintain high morale is prominent, likely a unique need to war and crisis situations, it can be quite challenging for refugees to keep their morale up because of not only the situations they are in, and but also violent, graphic media coverage (Kozman and Melki, 2017). This is especially problematic as refugee use ICTs and media to deal with boredom and an acute need to remain informed on the situation back home, drives social media use exceeding pre-crisis levels (Xu, & Maitland, 2016).

Organizations may communicate and amplify the range of social media posts by mixing targeted information with entertaining posts, and by inviting experts who can give advice to refugees on how to keep up their morale. For example, they can start encouraging refugees to share personal or family celebrations (e.g., weddings) or achievements (e.g., school graduation).

Surviving

ICT and media use help refugees and immigrants to survive psychologically and physically. Refugees and immigrants use media to gather information to help them avoid danger and feel safe (Kozman and Melki, 2017). For example, refugees need information to know whether a bomb had been dropped nearby or someone they knew was injured or killed.

In their work in a detention camp, Coddington and Mountz (2014) also found that access to information about families and friends outside helps detainees to survive bewildering periods of uncertainty and isolation, thus, helping them to be more resilient in the stressful situation they are in. Authors concluded that access to ICTs improves the integrity of the asylum system itself. Similar results were found by George (2017) with refugees in Rome.

While previous studies found that social media and phones empower refugees and immigrants, studies found many existing barriers to access to information communication technologies as well as demographic differences in use.

Barriers and individual differences

Studies found that there are demographic differences such as age, gender and education in how refugees use ICT and social media. Xu and Maitland (2016)'s field research in Za'atari Syrian refugee camp found that people who have higher education and who are generally older tend to own a mobile phone. While gender and English abilities do not have much effect on mobile phone ownership, women are most likely to own more than one SIM card, potentially as a communication gatekeeper for their families.

Cassar, Gauci, & Bacchi (2016) found that the use of social networks (e.g., Twitter, LinkedIn) other than Facebook is quite limited among asylum seekers in Malta. Other networks also tend to attract people with a higher level of education, and women are more likely to use Twitter and LinkedIn than men. This indicates that communication with migrants would be most effective through Facebook, but that when particular demographic groups are being targeted, other platforms will reach high numbers of readers and members.

Age is also found a significant predictor of content generation on new media (Kozman & Melki, 2017). Opposite to mobile phone ownership, younger people tends to use new media (for consumption and production) more than older and less-educated people. Similarly, Yap and Leffler's (2017) study of Syrian refugees in Lebanon found that Syrian youth had to share the current news with their parents whose digital literacies are not high enough to use social media themselves. In general, illiteracy and obstacles to access to new media and mobile telephones reduces the importance of social media for refugees (Kozman & Melki, 2017).

Wall et al. (2015) noted that mobile phone usage is vulnerable to technological issues such as accessing a connection, alternative SIM cards, and, perhaps most importantly, continued government surveillance. They further highlight that while mobile phone access is very important for refugees, the obstacles in getting these necessities, and the ways refugees' strategies to cope with information precarity were uneven and unpredictable. The refugees' unstable environment has indeed contributed to new vulnerabilities along with new practices to engage with these same obstacles in sometimes resourceful and creative ways. In a similar vein, Gillespie et al. (2016) found that another reason refugees are reluctant to share their true identities online is the fear of potential reprisals from organizations or governments that may be monitoring social media. When they share information online, they use fake identifications and avatars rather than their own images.

Language is also an important variable helping refugees and immigrants in their adaptation in their host countries. English language proficiency enables refugees to establish interpersonal relationships with members of the host culture. It also allowed them to use the host media to get the first-hand information about the host culture. Gillespie et al. (2016) recommends a multilingual engagement with refugee groups. These languages may include Arabic, English, Spanish, Turkish, German, Portuguese, and others.

ICT and Social Media Use in Humanitarian Aid

Technology plays an important role in the humanitarian work NGOs do around the world, including in areas where the larger numbers of incoming refugees and immigrants are documented. Emerging technologies, innovations and social media help humanitarian aid workers plan and deliver a better and more accurate response during and after disasters and wars. Some of the benefits of using ICTs by NGO are efficient information dissemination, paper reduction, and emotional support among the team (Chang, Liao, Wang, & Chang, 2010). Cloud-based remote management also reduces pressure on the network management skills of those personnel (Maitland & Bharania 2017).

Interactive technology increases NGOs' communication and facilitates networking by enhancing the core tasks of getting information to constituents, channelling and interpreting information from varied sources, aggregating information and demands, transmitting them to diverse audiences, and mobilizing individuals and groups (Bach and Stark 2014). NGO use of interactive technologies allows them to go beyond service provision and function as a global navigational resource for exploring a knowledge space full of uncertainties and unknowns. NGOs themselves transform when shift their emphasis from brokering information to facilitating knowledge (Bach and Stark 2014). Facilitating knowledge helps communities to support themselves and flourish.

Previous studies on the *effects* of ICT and social media use in recovery has found positive results. In the case of the 2011 Japanese earthquake and tsunami, the researchers found individual ICT and media use are associated with online civic participation, which in turn correlates with social capital for disaster recovery (Cheng et al.2015). Research by Madianou (2015) focused on recovery in displacement following Haiyan, found social media use hastened recovery of middle-class survivors, while lower socio-economic survivors lagged behind. The results demonstrate effects of ICT use in recovery reflect established social inequalities.

Alhayek (2016), examined the work of Syrian activists, from seven activist organizations, with Syrian refugee women in Jordan and the relationship between their online and offline activism in varying and highly specific ways according to the historical, social, and political contexts. On-the- ground activists use online media as a tool to garner support, and not mere online propaganda alone, to improve the lives of marginalized Syrian refugee women. These informal organizations secure funding through individual and unofficial donations, and ICTs offer these independent activists significant opportunities to network and fundraise. Activists build trust and sympathetic relationships with their donors by sharing their experiences through ICTs and by disseminating stories and visuals of people in need of assistance such as housing and healthcare. The members of informal organisations generally use technologies like mobile phones to record and/or photograph stories of the refugee women in need as a proof of their situations and then share the visuals and stories online via social media, especially Facebook, to reach more than 20,000 followers. They also use ICTs to network and secure funding for their offline activities such as distributing aid, medical care, and relocation of refugee women outside the refugee camps.

Overall, NGOs use ICT and social media to communicate information to refuges, and to inform public and raise awareness about humanitarian situations.

The Challenges of ICT and Social Media

If communication itself is a form of humanitarian aid, that implies an obligation to ensure as many people as possible have the opportunity to benefit from the presence of connectivity. Also, camp-based or other "digital divide" issues should be considered and mitigated. In a recent study, humanitarian staff revealed major challenges in meeting refugees' information and communication needs (Hannides et al. 2016). For example, they did not know when and whether borders would open to allow refugees to continue their journey. While they wanted to share helpful, accurate information, these agencies knew that the situation could quickly change, being outside their control. With multiple actors working in this space, and a rapidly changing situation, providing accurate, consistent information was, and remains, extremely challenging. Because information can disseminate quickly among refugees, sharing inaccurate information can disturb the trust refugees have towards NGOs. It is also likely that different social media tools can have different benefit for NGOs.

Tapia, Moore & Johnson (2013) investigated the use of microblogged data (e.g., Twitter) by disaster response and humanitarian relief organizations. The data collection was facilitated by NetHope.[8] Authors conducted in-depth interviews with representatives from participating member organization. They found that while microblogged data is useful to responders in situations where information is limited, such as at the beginning of an emergency response effort, in many situations the details and accuracy of data could not meet the standards of quality needed. This leads to varying levels of acceptance and use among organizations. They highlight the challenges of translating information provided by local with good intentions into actionable information by relief organizations due to trust. There are, however, benefits of microblogging to refugees as they become more

---

[8] http://www.irinnews.org/report/99127/syrian-aid-tech-age

situationally aware during disasters and coordinate to help themselves (Palen, Vieweg & Anderson, 2010).

Some of the challenges humanitarian organizations face are because of their organizational structures where there has been a centralised command system, standard operating procedures to ascertain appropriate responses to disasters. A central aspect of these organizational mechanisms is complete control over the internal flow of information concerning the crisis from source to organizational decision maker respectively. This ensures accuracy, security, legitimacy, and eventually, trust between the organization and information source. Despite a tremendous amount of research in the area, no mechanisms have been employed for harvesting microblogged data from the public in such a manner that facilitates organizational decisions. Crisis responders, on the other hand, never have perfect knowledge of any given crisis, as crises, by definition, are scenarios where conditions hinge on extreme instability (Palen et al. 2010).

Infrastructure can create barriers for further integration of ICT into NGO efforts. The majority of refugees reside in developing countries where the telephone network, internet network, and even the power grid are not fully developed. Moreover, accessing connectivity services (e.g., 3G) is expensive. This creates a barrier when NGOs aim to scale up technologies and tools in these contexts. An example case study was presented by Maitland & Bharania (2017). The authors studied how an NGO and two tech industries cooperated during the Syrian refugee crisis, with the results suggesting three outcomes. First, the network design and implementation were positively influenced by ongoing commitments, trust, and specialization, calling into question the extent to which 'hastily formed' applies in all contexts. The NGO plays a coordinating role as well as serves as a 'long term player in the market.' The tech companies trust the work of the NGO's staff due to their long-term relationship. This, in turn, allowed one of the tech companies to focus on the network's high-level design, reflecting specialization between the team participants. Second, the accumulated expertise and an assessment of the context made from a distance by the tech company designers drove decision-making concerning the integration of security features into the network's design. Third, deployment of communication networks is a multi-stage and ongoing task, with initial decisions made independently prior to deployment, and subsequent decisions made jointly both in the stage of network deployment but also during ongoing operations. These together show the difficulty NGOs face when they wanted to scale up technologies.

Resource constraints are also limiting factors for NGOs. Multiple tech communities have been motivated develop technologies for this context. They have organized numerous hackathons and formed specialized tech communities, such as Techfugees and EmpowerHack, that have rallied around different humanitarian causes. However, so far the resources are not developed enough to be scaled up and integrated with ongoing efforts of NGOs. In the long term, these technologies have been theorized to increase efficiency, cut down on costs of aid provision and ensure that the right people are getting the right aid. Due to high pressure nature of the work, some NGO staff may find flimsy ICT integration and have to redouble their efforts. Collaboration between IT professionals and NGOs can result in a more streamlined transition in adapting new technologies into NGOs' demanding work settings (Chang, Liao, Wang, & Chang, 2010).

Furthermore, there is a lack of governance at how refugees are represented by different activist organisations. Alhayek (2016) found that while ICTs can be used by activists to further their efforts at reform and to improve the lives of women, they can sometimes be misused to misrepresent feminist progress through the propagation of essentializing cultural and gender discourses.

Examples of Technologies Used in Humanitarian Aid

NGOs make extensive and innovative use of ICTs, including databases, laptops, and integrated point-of-sale terminals and biometric data systems, while not are equally beneficial to their goals. UNHCR official website listed a set of technologies that have been used by different NGOs. Among these are satellite mapping, biometric scanning, electronic food vouchers, SIM cards and QR codes (UNHCR 2017). While satellite mapping can be used to create detailed maps of areas of concern, biometric data can be used to register and identify refugees in final locations. For example, Syrian refugees arriving in Jordan were registered to a biometric database. In partnership with Cairo Amman Bank, refugees eligible for cash handouts from UNHCR can collect their money from over 100 locations in Jordan. Instead of using a debit card, they simply have their eye scanned at the ATM machine. Biometric scanning help agencies to map where refugees are and assess how long they have to travel to access the banking services.

In Turkey, the World Food Program, in conjunction with the Turkish Red Crescent Society, Kızılay, runs an electronic food voucher scheme. The refugees receive cards loaded up with 'credit' on a monthly basis with which they can shop for food in local shops. This not only gives the refugees choice of what they want to buy, but it also frees WFP from having to manage mass food distributions. Moreover, this arrangement eliminates the black marketization of free food items and provides more security than circulating hard currency. The e-Food Card is loaded with 80TL ($45) per person per month for use in shops selected by WFP, Kızılay and the government. Digitization also help WFP to collect data on refugees' needs based on the usage of the cards.

Through the use of special SIM cards, Syrian refugees can receive mass information messages and contact details of service providers which can make communication between the NGOs, service providers and refugees more streamlined. The SIM cards are fitted with emergency SMS features so that refugees can also make free calls to the UNHCR information line, which usually receives around 700 calls a day. The SIM cards do not expire, even if no credit is added to the account. Humanitarians aid workers use QR codes as a vital tool in getting essential aid to refugees who need it most. Other new technologies explored by NGOs include bitcoin and blockchain to transfer cash assistance to beneficiaries. Even drones are considered as a potential method of delivering aid packages to conflict areas.

Conclusion

ICT and social media are shifting the ways in which refugees and immigrants experience their journey. Once they arrive to their destinations, using social media may generate a sense of belonging in the new community that allow them to integrate their less mobile life as refugees with a wider array of daily activities and social possibilities. Studies imply that it is important to encourage refugees and recent immigrants to form interpersonal relationships with hosts which were found to positively contribute to refugees' cross-cultural adaptation process, and psychological well-being. Accordingly, resettlement agencies and others serving refugees should work on building programs, events and other opportunities where refugees can meet and form friendships with those from the host culture, allowing those relationships to extend to digital environments. Social media can play an integral role in this effort.

Migrants and refugees use social media as a tool for communication and social networking as well as a means of information distribution and reception. Because of the potential language barrier, agencies may use both refugees' native language and the language of the host county in their communication with refugees. Furthermore, as it was highlighted earlier, Facebook may be the most accessible social network application to reach these refugees because of it is the most commonly used one among refugees. Besides Facebook includes lots of features in one platform such texting, video chatting, picture sharing or video sharing. Facebook also enables refugees and immigrants to choose to which communities they will belong in online platform. This may create their sense of belonging and help to make their adaptation process easier and they can simply reach useful communities.

Since ICT and social media use by NGOs' facilitates flow of information, it has become very instrumental to reach their target groups. NGOs can communicate with refugees and immigrants faster and easier and they can affect more people. NGOs can determine refugees' and immigrants' needs and meet their requirements. Sometimes they organize aid campaigns for them through online social media platforms. With the pictures and videos of refugees and immigrants, donors create empathy and develop sympathetic relationships with the people in need of help. As ICT and social media allow quick access to audience, they have a power of organizing. NGOs mostly do that kind of sharing via their Facebook pages. Besides, they communicate friendly messages with refugees and immigrants; they rectify inaccurate information about refugees and immigrants and defend their rights through social media platforms. ICT use by NGOs also helps them to record refugees or immigrants or the numbers of aids. Since ICT facilitates to information flow inside NGOs, it eliminates bureaucratic challenges of helping process.

Unstable conditions about refugees and immigrants make it difficult to get right information to NGOs. Therefore, NGOs have challenges about accuracy of data they have to share. Besides there are many fake news at social media platforms that seem as if they are given by NGOs and cause misdirection for refugees and immigrants or create hostility among people of host countries. It can be very difficult to repair these impacts.

There are concerns about whether these technologies will end up distancing International NGOs and NGO workers from the refugee community with technology becoming the main mediator between them and refugees. Critics have also pointed out that the UNHCR's biometric system requires an already vulnerable population that fears prosecution to share data that they would not have been inclined to share if they did not have to in order to get aid. Furthermore, one of the worries is that if these systems fail, would people who should be receiving aid be denied it? Or, what are the dangers of tracking every action of these people's lives? While the technology has immense potential in improving the humanitarian system, we should remain critical and encourage the monitoring and evaluation of these new technologies on the short and long term. These evaluations should go beyond numbers and look at shifts in interactions between NGOs and refugee communities.

Lastly, future studies should focus on the use of diverse methodologies that were employed to assess refugees' online behaviours and attitudes. Such studies can help researchers structure meta-review papers and contribute to the field.

References

Alhayek, K. (2016). ICTs, Agency, and Gender in Syrian Activists' Work Among Syrian Refugees in Jordan. Gender, Technology and Development, 20(3), 333–351.

Bach, J., & Stark, D. (2004). Link, Search, Interact: The Co-Evolution of NGOs and Interactive Technology. Theory, Culture & Society, 21(3), 101–117. https://doi.org/10.1177/0263276404043622

Brunwasser, M. (2015, August 25). A 21st-Century migrant's essentials: Food, shelter, smartphone. The New York Times.

Cassar, C. M., Gauci, J.-P., & Bacchi, A. (2016). Migrants' use of social media in Malta. Retrieved from http://www.pfcmalta.org/uploads/1/2/1/7/12174934/social_media_report_08-2016_-_final.pdf

Charmarkeh, H. (2013). Social media usage, tahriib (migration), and settlement among Somali refugees in France. Refuge: Canada's Journal on Refugees, 29(1).

Chang, Y.J., Liao, R.-H., Wang, T.-Y., & Chang, Y.S. (2010). Action Research as a Bridge Between Two Worlds: Helping The NGOs and Humanitarian Agencies Adapt Technology to Their Needs. Systemic Practice and Action Research, 23(3), 191–202. https://doi.org/10.1007/s11213-009-9154-8

Cheng, J.W., Mitomo, H., Otsuka, T., Jeon, S.Y. (2015). The effects of ICT and mass media in post-disaster recovery – A two model case study of the Great East Japan Earthquake. Telecommunications Policy, 39(6), 515-532. https://doi.org/10.1016/j.telpol.2015.03.006

Chouliaraki, L. (2017). Symbolic bordering: The self-representation of migrants and refugees in digital news. Popular Communication, 15(2), 78–94.

Coddington, K., & Mountz, A. (2014). Countering isolation with the use of technology: how asylum-seeking detainees on islands in the Indian Ocean use social media to transcend their confinement. Journal of the Indian Ocean Region, 10(1), 97–112.

Definition of NGOs. (n.d.). Retrieved September 28, 2018, from http://www.ngo.org/ngoinfo/define.html

Deidenang, C. (2013). Today another group of new asylum seekers arrival at #Nauru international airport 25 males only of African origin seen disembark. Tweet. Oct 28.

Dolan, R., Conduit, J., Fahy, J., & Goodman, S. (2016). Social media engagement behaviour: A uses and gratifications perspective. Journal of Strategic Marketing, 24(3-4), 261-277.

Dotan, J., & Cohen, A. A. (1976). Mass media use in the family during war and peace. Communication Research. https://doi.org/10.1177/009365027600300403

George, T. V. (2017). 'As important to me as water': how refugees in Rome use smartphones to improve their well-being. Doctoral dissertation, Massey University.

Gillespie, M., Ampofo, L., Cheesman, M., Faith, B., Iliadou, E., Issa, A., ... & Skleparis, D. (2016). Mapping refugee media journeys: Smartphones and social media networks.

Hannides, T., Bailey, N., & Kaoukji, D. (2016). Voices of refugees information and communication needs of refugees in Greece and Germany. BBC Media Action.

Jones, G. and Wires. (2013, September 28). Coalition breaks silence on sunk boat after Tony Abbott flees reporters after asylum seekers drown on way to Australia.

Kozman, C., & Melki, J. (2017). News media uses during war: The case of the Syrian conflict. Journalism Studies, 1–23. https://doi.org/10.1080/1461670X.2017.1279564

Madianou, M. (2015). Digital inequality and second-order disasters: Social media in the typhoon haiyan recovery. Social Media + Society, 1(2), 205630511560338 https://doi.org/10.1177/2056305115603386

Maitland, C., & Bharania, R. (2017). Balancing Security and Other Requirements in Hastily Formed Networks: The Case of the Syrian Refugee Response. (SSRN Scholarly Paper No. ID 2944147). Rochester, NY: Social Science Research Network. Retrieved from https://papers.ssrn.com/abstract=2944147

Marlowe, J. M., Bartley, A., & Collins, F. (2017). Digital belongings: The intersections of social cohesion, connectivity and digital media. Ethnicities, 17(1), 85–102.

Palen, L., Vieweg, S., and Anderson, K. M. (2010). Supporting "Everyday Analysts" in Safety- and Time-Critical Situations. The Information Society, 27(1), 52–62.

Pfaff, J. (2010). Mobile phone geographies. Geography Compass, 4, 1433-1447.

Syrian aid in the tech age. (2013, November 14). Retrieved September 28, 2018, from http://www.irinnews.org/report/99127/syrian-aid-tech-age

Tapia, A. H., Moore, K. A., & Johnson, N. J. (2013). Beyond the trustworthy tweet: A deeper understanding of microblogged data use by disaster response and humanitarian relief organizations. In ISCRAM.

T.C. Başbakanlık Afet ve Acil Durum Yönetimi Başkanlığı. (2017). Türkiye'deki Suriyeliler Demografik Görünümü, Yaşam Koşulları ve Gelecek Beklentilerine Yönelik Saha Araştırması https://www.afad.gov.tr/upload/Node/25337/xfiles/17a-Turkiye_deki _Suriyelilerin_Demografik_Gorunumu_Yasam_Kosullari_ve_Gelecek_Beklentilerine_ Yonelik_Saha_Arastirmasi_2017.pdf

UN & Office for the Coordination of Humanitarian Affairs. (2013). Humanitarianism in the network age: including world humanitarian data and trends 2012.

Vertovec, S. (2009). Transnationalism. Routledge.

Wall, M., Otis Campbell, M., & Janbek, D. (2015). Syrian refugees and information precarity. New Media & Society, 1461444815591967.

What is ICT (information and communications technology, or technologies)? - Definition from WhatIs.com. (n.d.). Retrieved September 28, 2018, from https://searchcio. techtarget.com/definition/ICT-information-and-communications-technology-or- technologies

Xu, Y., & Maitland, C. (2016). Communication behaviours when displaced: A case study of Za'atari Syrian Refugee Camp, ACM Press, (pp. 1–4).

Yap, Y.-Y., & Leffler, A. (2017). A Communication Analysis for UNICEF Lebanon-A media landscape of Lebanon, media consumption habits of Syrian refugees and potential C4D interventions to promote social inclusion and child/youth protection for Syrian children and youths in Lebanon.

CHAPTER 7

REPRODUCTION OF DESIRE: OVERUSE OF SOCIAL MEDIA AMONG SYRIAN REFUGEES AND ITS EFFECTS ON THE FUTURE IMAGINATION

Barış Öktem

Introduction

Technological developments in the form of smart devices, such as the internet and smartphones, have been in our lives for more than a few decades. The internet as an advanced form of smart devices was once developed as a means of military and intelligence communication, but it has now transformed into one of the instruments of life used by four out of five of the world population (Schivinski & Dariusz, 2016).

Social networking sites (SNSs), operating on the Internet, have become a popular means of creating a virtual form of social relations with others (Giannakos et al., 2013). Use of social media is rapidly increasing day by day and has become widespread in many societies in the world, with particularly popular and well-known SNSs such as Facebook reaching 2.32 billion active users globally (Facebook, 2018). SNSs not only enable users to set up friendships, establish new relationships and connect with others, but also, as Boyd & Ellison (2007) state *"enable people to form their own individual profiles and present a rich set of information about themselves by providing information about their attitudes, activities, personalities, relationship status, daily habits"* (p.249).

Many recent studies (Nedkarni & Hofmann, 2012; Rosenberg & Egbert, 2011) have been done to investigate social media platforms, such as Facebook, Snapchat, and Instagram. This designed and well-considered SNSs profiles are more likely to demonstrate the self on the profile in an affirmative and positive variant by targeting positive reactions and attention of others (Vogel et al., 2015). In addition, many researchers have been setting sights on the field of social media in order to understand its effects on the tendency of users regarding various areas, such as electronic word-of-mouth (eWOM) (e.g. Smith & Pyle, 2015; Rezvani et al., 2012), online reviews (e.g. Karakaya & Barnes, 2010), virtual brand communities (e.g. Carlson et al., 2008; Brodie et al. 2013), social networking pages (e.g. Gensler et al., 2012),

The number of refugees across the world have started to radically increase especially after the wars in Afghanistan and Iraq, and, in last decades in Arab countries, due to civil war, revolution and political instabilities (Fargues & Fandrich, 2012). The number of refugees in 2005 in the world was approximately 12.5 million, the least number in the last few decades; however, the number of refugees since then has almost doubled (WorldBank, 2017). As of 2011, due to the burst out Syrian Civil War more than 6.5 million Syrians had to flee more than 20 countries and sought asylums. Moreover, more than 6 million Syrians displaced internally in their home country (UNCHR, 2018).

Even though numerous researches have been done on investigating the use of social media and its relations and effects on users (Tang et al., 2015; Berryman et al. 2018), there is a gap regarding on the refugee spaces as camps and its effects on the refugee on social media. Due to the notion of being a refugee that basically means that being held away from many social, economic and educational interactions in public, the refugee camps, shelters, and accommodations have become specific environments (Diken & Laustsen, 2002; Eyinc, 2015) as either encouragement/motivation or excuse for overuse of social media. Particularly, as an outcome of ethnographic research in the field, when those refugees who are on move to migrate from a place to another one, social media use increases in their daily lives (Dekker et al., 2018). One of the most common attitudes among refugees' daily habits during emigrating is being in touch and in contact with other refugees for several reasons, such as asking for secure places to each other (ibid); updating each other about their health and conditions (Wall et al., 2017); and asking questions regarding the places where they are and so forth.

In addition to using smartphones and the Internet prior to and during migration, the infrastructure of refugee camps plays crucial roles on the daily habits and behavior of refugees. Refugee camps mostly constructed as an isolated space from social interactions with various intentions that might protect vulnerable people from any threats (Black, 1998), protection of the collective identity of refugees (Diken, 2010), and controlling the integration process of refugees in daily lives (Feldman, 2007). However, technological instruments such as smartphones and the Internet encourage and motivate social media users to spend more time on in almost fully locked, controlled and monitored spaces such as, refugee camps. Subjected to the overuse of social media, many refugees have a tendency to do a social comparison with other Syrian refugees who arrived and settled in Western European countries. Social comparison of Self with Other, particularly in the limitation of information precarity, and biased and personally expressed information, might become either a push or pull factor (Schoorl et al., 2000) for many Syrian refugees who are in isolated and closed refugee camps.

This article aims to contribute an understanding to the relation between overuse of SNSs and effects of SNSs on the future imagination of Syrian refugees who stay in the refugee camps. Due to the nature of vulnerability of being displaced, in the frame of the Self and Other, Syrian refugees -as self- have started to desire the represented Western modernity, lifestyle and identity to them especially via SNSs by the Other Syrian refugees who arrived in Western countries. The overuse of SNSs among Syrian refugees in isolated and limited refugee camps and the content of SNSs as reflected and shared images and ideas have created biased and deficient assumptions regarding the destinations where most of the Syrian refugees started to desire. This research offers a perspective that constructed on the analysis of biased images, information precarity, and online posted thoughts of those refugees who arrived in destinated countries, mostly Western European.

Overuse of Smartphones and Social Media

Increase in use of smartphones and the Internet, as an inevitable part of the daily lives especially in the digital age/millennium (Kuss & Lopez-Fernandez, 2016), has been studied in the disciplines of sociology (Lupton, 2012), psychology (Eijnden et al., 2016), economy, and political sciences (Fuchs, 2018). In the wake of the invention of the telecommunication system, the advanced form of communication versions such as video calling and social media, have become diversified both as a need of social interactions of today, and also a new form of capitalist product (Hesmondhalgh, 2016). Recently, the SNSs is one of the most discussed and studied subjects by many scholars (Vogel et al. 2015; Yildiz Durak & Seferoglu, 2019.) The use of SNSs have an invisible impact on the perception and imagination of users as a side effect either to redirect and manipulate the tendency of users regarding online purchasing (Goodrich & de Mooij, 2014) or future imagination, envisioning of virtual reality (Klischewski, 2014) regarding the places, lifestyles, and identities represented by the Other users.

The structure and design of most SNSs are due to different reasons developed to encourage and motivate users to express positive side of their personalities and lives. The more SNSs users expressed themselves to be social on online, the more a positive biased tendency to use the SNSs platforms is cultivated. Yet the begin to use social media have mostly been motivated by satisfaction and pleasure which then becomes like a daily social habit in continuance usage of it (Hsiao et al, 2016: 343). The social habits through its nature trigger and encourage the person to repeat the action s/he did again without questioning the action consciously. Habits are defined as actions that are performed automatically in response to contextual indications that have been incorporated with (Wood & Neal, 2007). There are direct interaction and influences between habits and the habitat as social and physical space.

In this regards, as one of the main arguments of this paper, the reciprocal relationship of the use of SNSs as a social habit, -which naturally postpones the critique of the intensity of its usage, and impact of the surrounded and limited spaces, the refugee camps, on the persistence of this habit have a common intersection and relationship in between.

The Identity Formation of the Desire: The Self vs the Other

After the works of the Gilles Deleuze and Felix Guattari (1983, 2013) on the desire and its intersection with politics, which was as an introduction for the uninitiated subject, the desire in relation to politics has attracted the attention of many scholars (Goodchild, 1996). The desire has become one of the latest and most effective means targeted by capitalism and the means of production, especially the media by expanding it through marketing and advertising. The desire has been introduced via many scholars in various disciplines: "Desire is a powerful feeling of wanting or longing to have something, or wishing for something to happen in terms of sexuality, socio-economic career, social status and so forth" (Ruthrof, 1997; Buss, 2015; Tuck, 2010). Desire, in the context of Syrian refugees, has reciprocal action and reaction. While part of Syrian refugees in Western European countries are being the subject of re-production of desire; on the other side, social media user and opinion seeker Syrian refugees who stay in refugee camps are being indirectly objects of re-produced desire.

Jacques Lacan (2004) argued that the conflict between two identities utilizes into the development of *'being'* which mostly occurs between *Self* and *Other*. As soon as the conflict appears in between these identities, the Self immediately attempts to know and recognize the Other more in order to improve a defensive and protective personality mechanism, which is motivated via natural instincts. The perception of Self with respect to the Other, for instance, the desired/targeted destination countries and lifestyle by the Syrian refugees, is generated by smart devices, such as the Internet and SNSs nowadays.

A Syrian refugee staying in refugee camps in Turkey or Greece as a Self makes an attempt on to knowing Other Syrian refugee staying in Western European countries as Other. This mutual relationship through media appears with the unexposed wishes of those refugees who feel left behind. While a Syrian refugee arrives in Western European countries, the one stays behind practices his/her desire through the one who arrived with the instruments of social media; following the Other Syrian refugee' social media shares, posts, and reflections. This is the recreation of desire among Syrian refugees by themselves and within the force and limitation of refugee camps.

The image of Syrian refugees in the refugee camps or accommodations explicitly reveals the effect of overuse of SNSs on the Syrian refugees' daily lives. Syrian refugees while staying in these spaces, intrinsically have extra time and space for using SNSs. However, regardless the reasons of using SNSs, the images, ideas and reflections of Others on these SNSs platforms and websites constitute a biased and deficient perception and information precarity for those who use them. It should be noted that the conditions and environments, wishes and demands, desires and ambitions of refugees are that they want to move out from these spaces and re-establish a new life in order to physically and psychologically rehabilitate themselves. These wishes, desires, and ambitions are sketchily and incompetently constructed on the images and opinions and illustrated depictions on SNSs due to the lack of access to the reliable sources and information, by those who live in the places where most refugees want to arrive and settle. The point that I am trying to highlight is that there are unbalanced, and uncontrolled relations appear among Syrian refugees. Following the line, on the one hand, those Syrians who arrived in mostly Western European countries reflect and picture the image of high-quality life and opportunities which they have or not. On the other hand, those Syrians who are still on move or wish to move to arrive in these countries are being informed and directed by these reflections and images which I code as *'biased, deficient sources and information precarity'*.

It has been more than a year that I arrived here [Greece] and staying in this camp. I criticized myself a lot of times by questioning why did I come here? Because all people I know who went those countries [means Western European countries] passed through here and told me, advised me to do the same. They passed in a week time but as I said I am here one year! Now I cannot go back to Turkey again because I do not want to accept my failed attempt and do not want to live in Turkey too to be honest. So what I do now, my body lives in this camp but my mind is in those beautiful countries that I see on the internet... here is my advice for you, do not let any of your children to have smartphone or the internet, otherwise they might be like me, bodily in the room but mentally would be somewhere else [laughing] [Interviewee 26, Sounio Refugee camp, 15 November 2018]

Before coming to here [Germany], I was in touch with many of my friends and relatives who are in Germany. All of them were saying they are happy and have a good life. That is in a way true, the life conditions and opportunities are in Germany better especially in compare to life Turkey and Greece. However, for instance, I know many people who were in Jordan and Lebanon before and then came to Turkey and they were saying the life is in Turkey better than Jordan and Lebanon. It does not mean life in Turkey is really good, it depends where you compare with. If you consider life in Jordan in compare to Africa [means African countries], it is much better but not the ideal one... What I am trying to say is that people evaluate their daily conditions in comparison to worse places and desire a better one. Therefore, life in Germany is better than Greece, for example, but not as people express it to others. Also, you know what, I know you will not believe me, [smiles]

Syrians are interesting because they want to draw a false picture for other Syrians who are not in Western countries. I do not know why they are like this. I guess they feel maybe lucky or satisfied when they are aware that they have a better life than other Syrians [Interviewee 49, Berlin Schoeneberg Refugee Sites, 17 April 2019]

Regarding the images, identities and ideas created and reflected positively on especially social media about Western European countries among Syrian refugees have ties with the historical colonialism due to the impact of that times (Healy, 1997). The popularity, prestige, familiarity and historical background of these countries have been known since colonial times by colonized people. As Syria was a League of Nations mandate (Maksidi & Prashad, 2016), Syrian people still can recall the colonial times of their country. Specifically, Britain and French empires and their continuous version of governments still have a strong image in the mind of Syrians, particularly in terms of identity and lifestyle (Kargin, 2018). This colonization was negatively criticized and reacted back in the colonial times by the people of colonized regions (Mingolo, 1993); however, day by day the negativity and hardness of critiques have left its place into the positivity with admiration, desire, and hierarchical identity formation. In the context of Syrian refugee migration, the produced images and ideas regarding these countries have a strongly positive impact on the preference and future imagination of Syrians. Those Syrian refugees who arrived in Western European countries produce these images and ideas by taking photos and videos of "happy and positive moments, spaces and life in these countries" and sharing on SNSs. Therefore, on the one hand, the re-produced positive images and re-presented positive ideas regarding these countries, become the source and information among refugee communities. And on the other, those Syrian refugees who stay in refugee camps in Turkey and Greece are the consumer and opinion seekers via the use of the SNSs. Future imagination regarding the re-settlement of life of these refugees intrinsically is being constructed on the reflected images and ideas they consume as a result of overusing SNSs. In the balance of reproducing and consuming the images and ideas which already have a strongly positive provision and prejudice among Syrians after the colonial times, creates, controls and re-shapes the desire about these countries.

Social Media as a Social Comparison Instrument

SNSs ensures personally expressed information about others which can be used for social comparison for the users. Many scholars (Vogel et al., 2015; Giannakos et al., 2013) stated that most people use SNSs for the purpose of making social comparisons with Others in order to realize what they have and what they experience. As interviewee 49 expressed that those Syrians who arrived and started to establish a new life socially compare their situation and conditions with other Syrians in order to remind themselves that they have a better life. The social comparison may be a realization for the conditions and opportunities which people have but not aware of it. In that sense, social comparison, especially via the use of SNSs and expression of personal positive characters, might even play a role of psychological relieving.

In this part, rather than focusing on those Syrians who share their opinions via SNSs, this paper is more interested in the tendencies and opinions of those Syrians who are receivers of these opinions. In other words, it is a discourse on the spot to use that those Syrian refugees seek an opinion while they stay in refugee spaces but wish to move out as *opinion seekers*. In defining the term *opinion seekers* as Smith and Pyle (2015) described that *"individuals who [seek] information or opinions from interpersonal sources -in this case SNSs- in order to find out about and evaluate products, services, current affairs, or other areas of interest"* (p.302).

The SNSs are one of the public instruments to analyze that how Syrian refugees express their opinions about themselves and the places they live in, and how those Syrians who are in refugee places receive these opinions as opinion seekers. At this point, it should definitely be introduced that as Vogel et al., (2015) indicated two fundamental points regarding the interface between social comparison and social media, which are:

> *First, because of the rich and varied information posted about others [and the self-] on social media, people [users] should be quite interested in using social media for the purpose of social comparison. Second, because social comparison information tends to be upward [positive] on social media, it produces negative consequences for well-being and self-evaluation (p.250).*

By following the two points, first, for an awareness of social conditions, self-representation, self-esteem and self-evaluation in comparison with others, by partly agreeing with Vogel et al. (2015), it has respectable advantages to use SNSs for an evaluation and social comparison with highly positive profiles. As mentioned, highly positive profiles presented on SNSs may help a person to realize their self-conditions and make an effort to develop it accordingly. Second, the use of SNSs differs in the number of certain circumstances, such as refugee camps, because whatever presented on SNSs is open to misinterpretation due to the negative impacts of the environment on the perception. In addition, importantly, whatever presented on SNSs is biased and uncompleted for a full understanding. Refugee camps as an environment and condition may reproduce the vulnerability of those people who have been displaced from their homes. In regard to the use of SNSs and being exposed to highly positive represented profiles and characters for those users who are in vulnerable psychology and condition in refugee sites may cause negative and deficient evaluations. Therefore, the interface of social comparison and SNSs should be re-considered and recontextualized in the frame of the effects of social and physical conditions for the users as a receiver or opinion seeker.

Significantly, if SNSs users meticulously present specific positive self-characteristics of their lives and conditions on social media platforms (Feinstein et al., 2013), then social comparisons made based on the biased and information precarity shared on social network platforms might show an alteration from in-person social comparisons. One-sided and incomplete picture may create mostly upward social comparisons to those who are better off on some dimensions, such as economic status, social opportunities and psychological states (Vogel et al., 2015; 250).

As a sum, the studies on the reproduction of desire in relation to Syrian refugees, especially those who accommodate in refugee sites, and in relation to their perception, motivation and tendencies in migration and the influence of SNSs they use on their way to the desired places –Western European countries– have to be re-examined. Dekker et al., (2018) introduced the function of social media use and its impact regarding the migration routes as a mediating role to their decisions and methods. Social media plays crucial roles in the future imagination, particularly with high-level use of it in refugee sites.

Methodology

The fieldwork sample consists of the majority of men (N: 27) and about half of the sample consists of women (N: 24) [N refers to the initial of 'Number' that indicates to the conducted interviews]. The majority of the interviewees (N: 44) are between 19 to 40 years old age. About more than half of the respondents (N: 27) are higher educated (bachelors and above university degrees), 8 respondents are high school graduated and the rest of the respondents -except 1 who had no education at all- (N: 11) hold secondary and below school degrees.

In total 51 face to face in-depth interviews took place in various environments, including the public cafes, private rooms, meeting offices at the refugee accommodations and in the located cities, where are Kahramanmaras, Gaziantep, Diyarbakir, Mardin in Turkey; Lavrio, Sounio, and Athens in Greece, and Berlin in Germany. The semi-structured interviews and participant observations carried out in Turkey (N: 19) at Kahramanmaras Temporary Protection Center and in the cities of Gaziantep, Diyarbakir, and Mardin in the period of mid-September to the end of November 2018. The second part of fieldwork was in Greece (N:17) at the Lavrio and Sounio Refugee Camps and it was applied in the period of the beginning of the November to the beginning of December 2018. The last part of the fieldwork was conducted in Berlin, the capital city of Germany (N: 15) at five different refugee accommodation sites from the end of March until the end of April 2019. As a result, it can be said that these 51 interviews have been done in various cities in these countries.

Most of the interviews (N: 48) were applied in Kurmanji dialect of Kurdish, and Syrian Arabic dialect. The rest 3 interviews were conducted in English. As a researcher, I am qualified enough to speak Kurmanji and English in advance level; however, for those who only spoke Arabic, 1 Syrian female interpreter and more than 5 experienced Syrian interpreters conducted the interviews in Syrian Arabic dialect.

Table 1. Profiles of Interviewees

	Turkey	Greece	Germany
	n.19	n.17	n.15
Age (average)	30	30	30
18-28	8	9	9
29-39	5	6	3
40-50	6	2	3
Gender			
Male:	10	9	8
Female:	9	8	7
Marital status			
Single:	10	5	7
Married:	9	11	6
Divorced or Widow:	-	1	2
Education			
Secondary and below:	7	5	3
High school or equivalence:	3	2	3
Bachelor and above:	9	10	8

Table 1 demonstrates the profiles of Syrian refugees in three different countries with their average age group, gender, educational background, and marital status. Although interviewees were selected with the priority of gender, age group and educational, the final sample of interviewees should not be considered as the generalizable picture of Syrian refugees. The average duration of each interview lasted around 60 min, and all of the interviewees gave consent to audio-record the interviews. The interviews were set on the basis of semi-structured and open-ended questions.

Table 2. The Internet and Social Media Applications and Websites Consulted with Refugees

	Turkey (n:19)	Greece (n:17)	Germany (n:15)
	%	%	%
SNSs (Facebook, Instagram)	94	100	86
	100	100	93
Messaging and communicating (WhatsApp, Messenger, Viber)	89	88	60
Video Sharing (YouTube, Snapchat)	94	100	73
Search Engines (Google and others)			

The consulted interviewees of this research had access to a variety of social media applications, websites, and the Internet, primarily via smartphones. In the last section of the interview questions, interviewees were specifically asked the choices of social media applications and websites within the context of social media use. The Table 2 indicates the percentage of the interviewees' social media use, the internet and websites preferences and use with the specified and highlighted major/well-known applications and websites by distinguishing with various labels, such as SNSs, messaging and communicating applications.

For gathering in-depth understanding of use and content of the SNSs, as a participant-observer I asked each interviewee to look at their social media accounts profiles and timelines after asking their content for it. All interviewees agreed to show me their social media accounts, specifically Facebook and Instagram. The most timeline contents of the SNSs used by interviewees were about photos and videos with short descriptions and notes. The most theme of the photos and videos posted by Syrian community members who either in European countries or neighboring countries, such as Turkey, Jordan and Lebanon were a frame of daily moment. The common shots were that taken photos or videos in public parks, new settlement environment like a house, picnic, new bought things such as cars, celebrations, and entertainments so forth. Interviewees were specifically asked such questions that

> *"How do you interpret and perceive these images and shared opinions?" "How do you imagine and dream these opinion sharers especially based on the images posted on the SNS?" "What do you desire to have in your future imagination especially in settled life?"*

The average duration of each interview lasted around 60 minutes, and all of the interviewees gave consent to audio-record the interviews. The interviews were set on the basis of semi-structured and open-ended questions on four different centered subjects. At first, starting to ask more general and introductory questions about their *background,* including *education, socio-economic status, age, marital status.* Second and third parts of the interview questions were more set sights on their *migration routes,* opinions regarding *local* and *international authorities, governments, interpretation of the images* of the desired countries they wish to arrive and settle. The last chapter was focused on the use of *social media, the Internet, structuring their time* according to the spaces, such as refugee camps and their interpretation and opinions of the social media. Destination countries, desired places, desired lifestyles, effect of personal images and thoughts on social media platforms, time duration of use of smartphones were the keywords I asked during the interviews. During the participant observation, refugees' daily actions and habits were paid attention to have a common opinion for an understanding of use of internet, smartphones and social media in refugee camps.

The Effect of the Physical Restrictions of Refugee Camps on Syrian Refugees' Social Media Usage

In this paper, the concept of refugee accommodation, shelter, and camps play a crucial part concerning the gathered data via ethnographic research methods in these sites; in Turkey, Kahramanmaras Temporary Protection Center; in Greece, Lavrio and Sounio Refugee Camps, and Germany, refugee accommodations in Berlin.

Kahramanmaras Temporary Protection Center has established by the co-operation of the Turkish Government and European Union support for corresponding the Syrian refugee crisis in Turkey in between 2014-15 where more than 25,000 Syrian refugees still hosted. The protection center is located 20 kilometres far away from Kahramanmaras city center and it is isolated from public access. The protection center due to *'security'* reasons is under heavy surveillance of the Turkish army and police forces. The area is completely surrounded by walls and razor wires on top of it, and every single entry and exit is recorded by the special security forces on the digital recording system. Refugees can go out in between limited and determined time schedules that differs according to season. Refugees have limited activities to do for socializing, health facility, education and entertaining.

Lavrio and Sounio refugee camps in Greece are structurally very similar to Kahramanmaras Temporary Protection Center. Both refugee camps in total accommodate about 1,000-2,000 refugees, including Syrians, Iraqi, Turkish, Irani, Afghani, and Congolese. Lavrio refugee camp was constructed just next to the Aegean Sea on the coast with the co-operation of the United Nation and Greek government nearly 60 years ago. The camp is located in the south-eastern part of Attica region, 35 miles away from Athens. Lavrio refugee camp has one main entrance and two blocks of 2 and 3-storey buildings. The camp is surrounded by high walls. There was no security and recording regarding surveillance and monitoring. It was hosting around 400 refugees, mostly Kurds from Turkey, Syria, and Iraq. Sounio refugee camp is converted from a secondary school scout camp into refugee camps and the area was surrounded by razor wires. It has two main entrances. The administration and security checkpoints and international charity organizations and NGOs were established in the center of the camp. There was no recording system but security checks and controls. Sounio refugee camp hosted more than 600 people from various countries, mostly Syria, Iran, Iraq, Afghanistan, Congo and so forth.

Refugee accommodations in Berlin, Germany, are structurally very varied in terms of designs and the use of the spaces. There were almost 90 sites of collective refugee accommodations in Berlin which accommodate approximately 22,000 people. I visited and carried out the research at only five of them due to the limited time. All five accommodations are buildings that belonged to the government. Most buildings are residences in very various parts of Berlin. All residences have security, information desk, and administration office at the entrance. There was no registration and record of in and out of refugee in these places during the daytime. Each refugee site has the diverse capacity to host refugees, from 30 to 500 people.

Syrian Refugees: The Use of Social Media as a Way of Surviving

Conditions of refugee camps and despair and vague of refugees' future more likely cause to decrease the self-confident and cause false interpretation of what they see on the screen of smart devices. The habitus of refugee camps not only affects the physical living conditions of refugees, and also it affects the psychology and well-being of refugees. Vogel et al. (2015) stressed the importance of well-being in the frame of the use of SNSs. Well-being might be highlighted, in comparison to those Syrian refugees who established a life in West (European) countries and its representation on SNSs, with those other Syrian refugees who feel left behind. In other words, the possible imaginations and opportunities based on the reflections and projections of Syrians who settled in economically better conditioned western European countries with a high degree of probability impress Syrians who are in a bad living condition. Since Syrians stay in refugee camps naturally compare themselves either socially or economically with other Syrians who demonstrate that they have a mostly positive life, this social and psychological comparison might lead to misinterpretation of reality. The reality is that those Syrians settled in better conditions places have not directly passed or upgraded their lives from bad conditions to better conditions. However, as stressed a few times that the nature and design of social media platforms encourage users to express the positive characters rather than the distress and troubles in which they still possibly have.

There is nothing to do but the internet and using phones. No work, no proper life, no obligation, so what would you do at that time? I use phone all the times to be honest, sometimes I need to charge my phone more than twice during the day [smiles]…When I am on the internet, I spend time on Facebook, Instagram, and WhatsApp, I mean mostly. I should also mention the YouTube and Messenger. Sometimes we watch online movies on the phones, what else can we do, when you have time and nothing specifically to do as a job or obligation? [Interviewee 4, Kahramanmaras Temporary Protection Center, 1 October 2018]

Dekker at al. (2018) drew attention on that

"the information precarity which is a state in which asylum migrants' access to news and personal information is insecure, unstable, and undependable, leading to potential threats to their well-being. In the case of social media, information precarity is caused by limited access, and diminished trustworthiness of social media information" (p. 3).

Social media consumers/users are not passive but take an active role in interpreting data and including media into their daily lives. In that sense, Katz (1959) had shown an insight and alternative approach through focusing on what motivates users for continued use of the media, instead of the direct message itself by asking *'what people do with media'* rather than *'what media does to people'* (p.2). The approach proposes that people use the media to fulfill specific gratifications (Giannakos et al., 2013; 595). Psychological well-being of Syrian refugees by the overuse of SNSs cover in the possible future imaginations in regard to extending the restrictions of refugee camps. It should be recalled that Syrian refugees should not be compared with a *'normal social media user'* who has not been in a limited social and physical environment. Rather than focusing on social and psychological satisfaction via being an active user on SNSs, the inevitability of the use of SNSs in certain circumstances is more important to attract attention.

One of the interview questions that *'What would you do if you did not have the opportunity to have internet and social media?'* have been respondent by many interviewees as following:

My phone is my everything now, it was not used to be. Here, in the camp this [shows the smartphone] is the gate to outside. I learn what is going on about my family, people and country. I am online all the time, except when I sleep [smiles]. I never counted but definitely [doing a quick calculation] more than 8 hours, yes even more than that. My favorite is Facebook and Instagram, you can see your people, their photos and where they are, what they say and share. Now we [refers to Syrians] are a digital community in everywhere [smiles] [Interviewee 26, Sounio Refugee Camp, 16 October 2018].

To be able to arrive here [Berlin, Germany], Facebook, Google Maps, YouTube, WhatsApp and other social media applications helped a lot. I cannot even imagine what would I do without internet. Definitely the internet is the main guide and advisor for millions of Syrians and for other people too in their lives [Interviewee 39, Tempelhof Refugee Site, 03 April 2019]

Thanks to the flexibility of time schedule and use of space in refugee accommodations in Berlin, most interviewees stated that they spend time in the city during the daytime for several purposes. While being social and busy with part-time works, language educations, and entertaining programs organized by the charity organization, NGOs and local councils distract refugees during the daytime as to not overuse their smartphones and the Internet. However, during the evening and night times, expressed by many refugees during the research, they use social media and the Internet in general. The Internet use on a phone was more than 2-3 hours among interviewed refugees in Berlin, which is less than those refugees in Turkey and Greece but more than an average social media user. In addition, it should be noted that the answers given by refugee interviewees regarding the duration of social media use are estimated numbers, and they most probably count the time that they spend on the internet and social media at once or consistently, not as a total duration of separate parts during the day.

I do not know to be honest, I used to use it too much. But since I arrived here, you know how German government is crazy about paperwork and documentation, I have been busy and distracted by the things I had to do. Now I mostly use social media during the evening, before going to sleep [smiles]. I usually spend time on Facebook and Instagram, and WhatsApp if you count as social media too... I was used to check my friends and relatives in other countries, but now I check for those who stayed behind and want to come here! [Interviewee 41, Berlin Tempelhof Refugee Sites, 4 April 2019]

Power of Images: Transformation of Text-Based Sources into Visually Oriented Sources

According to Boyd & Ellison (2007), social network sites are "web-based services that allow individuals to (1) construct a public or semi-public profile within a bounded system, (2) articulate a list of other users with whom they share a connection, and (3) view and traverse their list of connections and those made by others within the system" (p. 211). While doing this, recently the most common tendency to express the persona and profile via social networks sites (Instagram, YouTube, Dailymotion) have become a visual expression and image manufacturing. Image Manufacturing is the practice of constructing or performing an idealized cultural image which each user may manifest it differently (Smith & Pyle, 2015: 35).

> *First of all, the internet is one of the inevitable components of our reality and lives, not only for refugees but also for many people. Because the internet is the main window that opens our perspectives and daily lives to everything. It updates and renews our knowledge. I would definitely say that the internet is the most common teacher of everybody nowadays [smiles]. For us [means refugees] the internet and especially social media are inevitable in order to navigate ourselves to find out the ways to migrate, also, regarding the destination countries where we go. For example, we use it to be able to know what kind of life is going on in these places. I personally use YouTube often to reach out information about lives out there, it provides visual images and shows how life is in reality! [Interviewee 27, Sounio Refugee Camp, 15 November 2018]*

As interviewee 27 stresses the importance of visual sources by referring the use of *YouTube* which is a website for uploading images and videos, the impact of visually oriented sources on SNSs on the consumer/user is more effective than text-based sources (Vedantam et al., 2015). Smith & Pyle (ibid) indicates the transformation of content generation from text to eWOM that *"Within the past decade, consumers using social media have engaged in visual eWOM content generation, adding pictures to, or simply using pictures alone, as a form of communication (e.g., Instagram, Pinterest, Tumblr, etc.), and developing video content (e.g., YouTube, Dailymotion, etc.) to share their consumption experiences. This is a significant departure from the text-based online reviews in forums such as Amazon and e-Pinions, which typically share a common element"* (p.4). While text-based information requires an interpretation and effort for coming through an idea about it, the visual-based sources do not require a specific effort but only watching and following up the storyline to reach an idea about the content. Smith & Pyle (ibid), also remarks that *"as with the classical text-based eWOM, there is an obvious level of physical and psychological detachment between the opinion provider and the opinion seeker on media"* (p.5). On the one hand, the decision-making process historically within the interaction of social via text-based information/sources and opinion seekers' consumption required a 'rational' process of information and social comparison of the self. The last decade transformation of text-based information into visuals, on the other, such as photos, videos on the social interactive digital platforms changed the prototypical way of decision-making and social comparison.

In the context of the power of images as an impact on the users/consumers should be evaluated in the topic of refugees' use of SNSs, which this paper proposes that there is a false and lack representation of realities. Concerning the fact that the nature and structure of SNSs, it has decided impression on the expression of the Self, and the visual images as a representation of persona or thing have powerful indications on the opinion seekers. This failure to the fulfillment of representation of the image that introduces a content by opinion provider may trigger that those consumers/users who might deficiently interpret the represented content.

Conclusion

This research contributes toward developing literature in the field of social networking sites (SNSs) and its direct relation with space, such as refugee accommodations. SNSs is a new way of being social on virtual networks from long distances (Zeng et al., 2010) with increasing daily use. This increase of internet usage and SNSs, such as Facebook, Instagram, YouTube, WhatsApp are very common among Syrian refugees in order to keep pace and updates with news.

For this study, long-term fieldwork was conducted in refugee accommodations in Turkey, Greece, and Germany in order to understand the effect of social media effects on the future imagination and perception of Syrian refugees. In addition, the relationship between the use of SNSs and the refugee spaces is one of the main outcomes of this paper, which proposes that the restricted and isolated nature of refugee sites have a direct impact on the increased use of social media for several purposes. While the use of SNSs in refugee sites in Turkey and Greece were very high due to high restriction of the spaces with the rate of 95 percent among Syrian refugees, the reduced limitation and greater access to public spaces in Germany resulted in a drastically reduced rate of 78 percent. Usage of SNSs among Syrian refugees in Turkey and Greece was more than five hours, but just three hours in Germany.

This study claims that the high level of the use of SNSs has a direct link with the expectations of Syrian refugees regarding the future imaginations and resettlement places. Western European countries were the main destination and desire of Syrian refugees who were staying in refugee camps in Turkey and Greece. The shared and represented images and opinions by Syrian refugees arrived in Western European countries have created a deficient and biased perception and imagination about these places for those Syrian refugees staying in Turkey and Greece and desiring to arrive in these places. Therefore, the decreased level of the use of SNSs in Germany is one of the consequences of this reason that those Syrian refugees use SNSs less than other Syrians staying in refugee camps. This is because Syrian refugee settled in Western European countries do not seek further migration, and correspondingly, they do not need to use SNSs with the same way. Dekker et al. (2018: 2) and other scholars (Thulin & Vilhelmson, 2014; Engbersen,

& Faber, 2016) have strikingly shown that "migrants, particularly Syrian refugees' use of smartphones and social media prior to and during migration has grown in recent years. Social media have become popular channels of communication that make prospective migrants more informed about possibilities to migrate and destinations to settle". The internet-based platforms, applications, and websites on smartphones create an opportunity to access to strategic and crucial information that is disclosed via social media that can be beneficial prior to and during migration.

However, the high level of the use of SNSs had an indirect and invisible impact on the desire of the Syrian refugees. Although the studies on the directive and router function of media on the consumers/users have been studied by many scholars (Vogel et al., 2015; Smith & Pyle, 2015; Bruhn et al., 2012), the influence of SNSs on the perception of refugees regarding the desired destinations for re-settlement and establishing a life has been missing in the literature. The desire politics (Deleuze and Guattari, 1983, 2013; Goodchild, 1996) should be taken into consideration when especially evaluating the refugees' desire for the destination places. The social media representations, images, thoughts, and advice might trigger misinterpretation and deficient understanding of the shared content on the digital-based platforms. Particularly, in the context of the conflict between the Self and the Other this misinterpretation and deficient understanding should be taken into consideration when the desire of Syrian refugees about the destination places is investigated.

The information precarity is one of the common themes of social media researches. As Wall et al. (2017) speak of a situation about the biased and lack contents shared on social media by referring to issues that not only of access to social media information but also of trustworthiness of social media information. In addition, the transformation of the sources on the Internet from text-based information to visually oriented sources have created less questioning and examining the trustworthiness of the information. Publicly available and accessible information on SNSs, which comes from unknown sources, is less trusted and often named and labeled as *rumors*. Dekker et al. (2018: 9) state that the accessible and available information on social media in migration networks includes unverified, unconfirmed and instrumentally relevant statements which can be characterized as *rumors* (see DiFonzo & Bordia, 2007). Following the topic, the rumors shared on social network websites/applications are most likely to be broadcasted by both governments and mass media sources which mostly based on individual experiences, including irregular and false information (Bakewell & Jollivet, 2016). Beside that refugees are mostly conscious and aware of the uncertain and unverified information on SNSs (Burrell, 2012; Emmer et al., 2016). However, most interviewees stated that during the interviews that *they are very dependent on this type of information as it is very necessary for their life particularly during the migration.*

Social media networks have become an inevitable and necessary source of information for nowadays' refugees' reality. Refugees often access and use social media networks, applications and platforms, and online information for several reasons. However, it must be kept in mind that the very high level of the use of SNSs has been caused by other reasons as well rather than simply the preferences of the Syrian refugees. For instance, the nature of refugee accommodations due to the lack of socio-economic interactions in daily lives re-forms the use of time and preference of the refugees who stay in these places. The inevitability of the Internet, especially among Syrian refugees, motivates them to keep themselves active and aware of the news, happenings, and relationships.

References

Bakewell, O. & Jollivet, D. (2016). Broadcasting Migration Outcomes, in *O. Bakewell, G. Engbersen, M. L. Fonseca & Horst, C. (Eds.), Beyond Networks (pp. 183-204)* Feedback in International Migration. Basingstoke: Palgrave MacMillan.

Berryman, Chloe, Ferguson, Christopher J. & Negy, Charles (2018). Social Media Use and Mental Health among Young Adults, *Psychiatry Q (2018) 89*:307–314.

Boyd, D., & Ellison, N., (2007). Social Network Sites: Definition, History, and Scholarship [online] *Journal of Computer-Mediated Communication, 13* (1).

Brodie, R. J., A. Ilic, B. Juric, an&d L. Hollebeek (2013). Consumer Engagement in a Virtual Brand Community: An Exploratory Analysis, *Journal of Business Research 66* (8): 105–114.

Bruhn, M., V. Schoenmueller, & Schafer, D. B. (2012). Are Social Media Replacing Traditional Media in Terms of Brand Equity Creation? *Management Research Review 35* (9): 770–790.

Buss, David M. (2016). *The Evolution of Desire*, Springer International Publishing

Carlson, B. D., T. A. Suter, & T. J. Brown (2008). Social Versus Psychological Brand Community: The Role of Psychological Sense of Brand Community, *Journal of Business Research 61* (4): 284–291.

De Vries, L., S. Gensler, & P. S. H. Leeflang (2012). Popularity of Brand Posts on Brand Fan Pages: An Investigation of the Effects of Social Media Marketing, *Journal of Interactive Marketing 26* (2): 83–91.

Dekker, Rianne, Engbersen, Godfried, Klaver, Jeanine, & Vonk, Hanna (2018). Smart Refugees: How Syrian Asylum Migrants Use Social Media Information in Migration Decision-Making, *Social Media and Society January-March,* (1– 11).

Dekker, R., Engbersen, G., & Faber, M. (2016). The Use of Online Media in Migration Networks, *Population, Space and Place, 22,* 539–551.

Deleuze, Gilles & Guattari, Felix (1983). *Anti-Oedipus: Capitalism and Schizophrenia*, University of Minnesota Press Minneapolis.

Deleuze, Gilles & Guattari, Felix (2013). *A Thousand of Plateaus*, Bloomsbury Press.

Di Fonzo, N., & Bordia, P. (2007). *Rumour Psychology: Social and Organizational Approaches*, Washington, DC: American Psychological Association

Diken, Bulent & Laustsen, Carsten Bagge (2002). Camping as a Contemporary Strategy- From Refugee, *AMID Working Paper Series 32*/2003.

Emmer, M., Richter, C., & Kunst, M. (2016). *Flucht 2.0. Mediennutzung durch Flüchtlinge vor, während und nach der Flucht* [Flight 2.0. Media Use by Refugees Before, During and After the Tlight]. Berlin, Germany: Freie Universität Berlin.

Eyinc, Senem Sidal (2015). *Tasarim Yoluyla Multeci Barinma Sorununun Yonetimi: Izmir'deki Suriyeli Multeciler Ornegi,* Istanbul Teknik Universitesi, Fen Bilimleri Enstitusu.

Feinstein B, Hershenberg R, Bhatia V, Latack J, Meuwly N, & Davila J. (2013). Negative Social Comparison on Facebook and Depressive Symptoms: Rumination as a Mechanism, *Psychol Pop Media Cult;2*(3):161–70.

Fuchs, Christian (2018). Social Media and the Capitalist Crisis, *book chapter in The Media and Austerity: Comparative Perspectives,* 211-225, Routledge

Giannakos, Michail N., Chorianopoulos, Konstantinos, Giotopoulos, Konstantinos, &Vlamos, Panayiotis (2013). Using Facebook out of Habit, *Behaviour & Information Technology,* 2013 Vol. 32;6, 594–602. http://dx.doi.org/10.1080/0144929X.2012.659218

Goodchild, Philip (1996). *Deleuze and Guattari: An Introduction to the Politics of Desire,* London: Sage

Goodrich, Kendall & de Mooij, Marieke (2014). How 'Social' Are Social Media? A Cross-cultural Comparison of Online and Offline Purchase Decision Influences, *Journal of Marketing Communications, 20:*1-2, 103-116. DOI: 10.1080/13527266.2013.797773

Hesmondhalgh, David (2017). Capitalism and the Media: Moral Economy, Well-being and Capabilities, *Media, Culture & Society 2017, Vol. 39*(2) 202– 218.

Hsiao, Chun-Hua, Chang, Jung-Jung, & Tang, Kai-Yu (2016). Exploring the Influential Factors in Continuance Usage of Mobile Social Apps: Satisfaction, Habit, and Customer Value Perspectives, *Telematics and Informatics 33;* 342–355.

Karakaya, F. & Barnes, N. G. (2010). Impact of Online Reviews of Customer Care Experience on Brand or Company Selection, *Journal of Consumer Marketing 27* (5): 447–457.

Katz, E. (1959). Mass Communications Research and the Study of Popular Culture: An Editorial Note on a Possible Future for This Journal, *Studies in Public Communication, 21*-6. Retrieved from http://repository.upenn.edu/asc_papers/165

Klischewski, Ralf (2014). When Virtual Reality Meets Realpolitik: Social Media Shaping the Arab Government–citizen Relationship, *Government Information Quarterly 31;* 358–364.

Kuss, Daria J. & Lopez-Fernandez, Olatz (2016) Internet Addiction and Problematic Internet Use: A Systematic Review of Clinical Research, *World J Psychiatry March 22;* 6(1): 143-176.

Lacan, Jacques (2004). *The Four Fundamental Concepts of Psychoanalysis,* Karnac Books.

Lee, W.K. (2014). The Temporal Relationships among Habit, Intention and Issues, *Computers in Human Behavior 32:*54–60.

Lupton, Deborah (2012). *Digital Sociology: An Introduction,* Sydney: University of Sydney.

Wall, Melissa, Madeline Otis Campbell & Dana Janbek (2017). Syrian Refugees and Information Precarity, *New Media and Society, Vol. 19*(2) 240– 254, SAGE.

Nadkarni, A., & Hofmann, S. G. (2012*). Why Do People Use Facebook? Personality and Individual Differences, 52;* 243–249.

Fargues, Philippe & Fandrich, Christine (2012). Migration after the Arab Spring, *MPC Research Report 2012/09,* Migration Policy Centre (MPC) Research Report.

Rezvani, M., H. K. Hoseini, & Samadzadeth, M. M. (2012). Investigating the Role of Word of Mouth on Consumer Based Brand Equity Creation in Iran's Cell-Phone Market, *Journal of Knowledge Management, Economics and Information Technology February (8):* 1–15.

Rosenberg, J., & Egbert, N. (2011). Online Impression Management: Personality Traits and Concerns for Secondary Goals as Predictors of Self-presentation Tactics on Facebook, *Journal of Computer-Mediated Communication, 17;* 1–18.

Ruthrof, Horst (1997). The Politics of Desire, *Social Semiotics, 7:*2, 247-251, DOI: 10.1080/10350339709360384

Schivinski, Bruno & Dabrowski, Dariusz (2016). The Effect of Social Media

Communication on Consumer Perceptions of Brands, *Journal of Marketing Communications, 22*:2, 189-214, DOI: 10.1080/13527266.2013.871323

Schoorl, Jeannette, Heering, Liesbeth, Esveldt, Ingrid, Groenewold, George, van der Erf, Rob, Bosch, Alinda, de Valk, Helga, & de Bruijn, Bart (2000) *Pull and Push Factors of International Migrations,* European Communities.

Smith, Andrew N. & Martin M. Pyle (2015). A Video is Worth 1000 Words: Linking Consumer Value for Opinion Seekers to Visually Oriented eWOM Practices, *in Claudiu V. Dimofte, Curtis P. Haugtvedt, and Richard F. Yalch (eds.), Consumer Psychology in a Social Media World,* New York: Routledge

Tang, Jih-Hsin, Chen, Ming-Chun, Yang, Cheng-Ying, Chung, Tsai-Yuan, & Lee, Yao-An (2015). Personality Traits, Interpersonal Relationships, Online Social Support, and Facebook Addiction, *Telematics and Informatics 33* (2016); 102–108.

Thulin, E. & Vilhelmson, B. (2014). Virtual Practices and Migration Plans: A Qualitative Study of Urban Young Adults, *Population, Space and Place, 20,* 389–401.

Tuck, Eve (2010). Breaking up with Deleuze: Desire and Valuing the Irreconcilable, *International Journal of Qualitative Studies in Education,* 23:5, 635-650,

Van den Eijnden, Regina J.J.M., Lemmens, Jeroen S., &Valkenburg, Patti M. (2016). The Social Media Disorder Scale, *Computers in Human Behavior 61*; 478-487.

Vedantam Ramakrishna, Lin, Xiao, Batra, Tanmay, Zitnick, C. Lawrence, &Parikh, Devi (2015). *Learning Common Sense Through Visual Abstraction,* https://www.cv-foundation.org/openaccess/content_iccv_2015/papers/Vedantam_Learning_Com mon_Sense_ICCV_2015_paper.pdf (accessed on 9 June 2019)

Vogel, Erin A., Rose, Jason P., Okdie, Bradley M., Eckles, Katheryn, & Franz, Brittany (2015). Who Compares and Despairs? The Effect of Social Comparison Orientation on Social Media Use and Its Outcomes, *Personality and Individual Differences 86*; 249–256.

Wood, Wendy Helen & David T. Neal. (2007). A New Look at Habits and the Habit-goal Interface, *Psychological review* 114, 4: 843-63.

Yildiz Durak, H. & Seferoglu, S. S. (2019). Modeling of Variables Related to Problematic Social Media Usage: Social Desirability Tendency Example, *Scandinavian Journal of Psychology, 60,* 277–288.

Zeng, Danie, Chen, Hsinchun, Lusch, Robert, & Li, Shu-Hsing (2010). Social Media Analytics and Intelligence, IEEE *Computer Society- November/December,* 13-16.

www.ingramcontent.com/pod-product-compliance
Lightning Source LLC
Chambersburg PA
CBHW070345270326
41926CB00017B/4000